PEACOCK BOOKS

SHAKESPEARE SUPERSCRIBE

Does the thought of a looming English Literature exam fill you with depression and boredom . . .? Then *Shakespeare Superscribe* can help you.

Shakespeare Superscribe is an imaginative, enthusiastic approach to the study of Shakespeare's plays. Based on the highly successful series by London's Capital Radio, the book gathers – from distinguished actors, actresses, directors, critics and teachers – a miscellany of opinions, ideas and reminiscences which release 'set' texts from their tedious and inflexible exam limits. Instead of learning-by-heart you'll learn by interest and enthusiasm, by forming your own views on the plays.

The texts discussed here are *Romeo and Juliet, Macbeth, Julius Caesar, A Midsummer Night's Dream, Twelfth Night, The Merchant of Venice, Richard II* and *Henry IV (Part I)*, but whichever set book you are studying you'll enjoy discovering the possibility of such a variety of views and find the different interpretations of one work thought-provoking and stimulating to your own learning.

Shakespeare Superscribe

Transcripts from Capital Radio's
Set Books series

Edited with explanatory
background text by Myra Barrs

With a foreword by Maggie Norden

PENGUIN BOOKS
A PEACOCK BOOK

Penguin Books Ltd, Harmondsworth, Middlesex, England
Penguin Books, 625 Madison Avenue, New York, New York 10022, U.S.A.
Penguin Books Australia Ltd, Ringwood, Victoria, Australia
Penguin Books Canada Ltd, 2801 John Street, Markham, Ontario, Canada L3R 1B4
Penguin Books (N.Z.) Ltd, 182–190 Wairau Road, Auckland 10, New Zealand

Published in Peacock Books 1980
Background text copyright © Myra Barrs, 1980
Radio transcripts copyright © Capital Radio, 1980
Foreword copyright © Maggie Norden, 1980
Ian McKellen's contribution copyright © Ian McKellen, 1980
All rights reserved

Made and printed in Great Britain
by Hazell Watson & Viney Ltd,
Aylesbury, Bucks
Set in Monotype Ehrhardt

Except in the United States of America,
this book is sold subject to the condition
that it shall not, by way of trade or otherwise,
be lent, re-sold, hired out, or otherwise circulated
without the publisher's prior consent in any form of
binding or cover other than that in which it is
published and without a similar condition
including this condition being imposed
on the subsequent purchaser

Contents

A note on the text

The edition of Shakespeare's plays used throughout this book is the New Penguin Shakespeare.

Foreword

'Switched-on swot' – that's what I was labelled after producing Capital Radio's *Set Books* series for Hullabaloo. In fact, the idea came to me after talking to an assortment of dismally switched-off swots. Every year on Hullabaloo I run a phone-in on exams, and one thing I couldn't help noticing was how depressed many callers were at the prospect of the English Literature paper. So few of them seemed to find any enjoyment or relevance in the books they had been set. For many the texts represented little more than an interminable slog of 'key quotes' and learning-by-heart. So I cast about for some way that radio could be used to inject some excitement and enthusiasm into exam reading.

The solution I came up with was 'Superscribes'. By enlisting the help of distinguished actors, actresses, directors, authors and teachers, we would construct a 'collage' around each book; a miscellany of opinions, ideas and reminiscences which we hoped by their very variety would provide evidence that the word 'set' in Set Books doesn't necessarily mean 'rigid, inflexible'.

Once it had been put to these famous personalities that the essence of each collage was to stimulate interest in literature, to help lighten the sheer grind of studying, the response was terrific: concerned, inventive and generous.

The material was collected in all sorts of places. When I was lucky, contributors popped into the studio. If I was less fortunate, I'd lug my tape-recorder into a theatre dressing-room where, between appearances, an actor would sit down and think out loud into my mike about the intricacies of some classic role he'd had to familiarize himself with. The enthusiasm the contributors conveyed was infectious. With Shakespeare's plays, our 'cast' often suggested modern parallels, lending relevance and immediacy to daunting texts. I remember giving Ian McKellen a cup of coffee and asking, 'How can we wake up some of Shakespeare's sleepier stuff?' He replied by reciting the *Romeo and Juliet* prologue, changing the word 'Verona' to 'Belfast'. Donald Sinden donated a delightful memory of how he found the right 'face' for Malvolio by studying Graham Sutherland's yellow portrait of Somerset Maugham, and Peter Ustinov demonstrated how the plays might even be parodied. Making his debut as a Shakespearean critic was John Cleese, who volunteered to talk about *Twelfth Night*. He went home, made copious notes, then came back with a suggestion – supported by textual evidence – that Shakespeare was probably a bit pushed for time when he wrote it.

My thanks go to all of them for helping me, Capital Radio and any number of young furrowed foreheads among our listeners. If we had any overriding rule for the series, it was Ian McKellen's tip – 'Never trust anything – find out for yourself.' So an extra special thank-you to my researcher, Jill Freeman, whose diligence in carrying out that credo went beyond any call of duty.

And a final fond thanks must also go to Michael Aspel, for lending his comely ear to our tapes and running his discerning eye over our scripts.

MAGGIE NORDEN

Acknowledgements

The author and publishers would like to thank the following for permission to use copyright material: B. T. Batsford Ltd for extracts from *Prefaces to Shakespeare* by Harley Granville-Barker; Cambridge University Press for an extract from *Shakespeare's Stagecraft* by J. L. Styan; Curtis Brown Ltd on behalf of the Estate of Sir Arthur Quiller-Couch for an extract from *Shakespeare's Workmanship* by Sir Arthur Quiller-Couch; *The Daily Telegraph* for 'Brook Break-Through in "*Dream*" ' by John Barber; Faber and Faber Ltd and Random House, Inc., for an extract from *The Dyer's Hand* by W. H. Auden; Hamish Hamilton/Jonathan Cape for an extract from *Diaries of a Cabinet Minister* by Richard Crossman; William Heinemann Ltd, Harcourt Brace Jovanovich, Inc., and Mary McCarthy for an extract from *Venice Observed* by Mary McCarthy; Macmillan, London and Basingstoke, for an extract from 'The Rejection of Falstaff' by A. C. Bradley; Methuen & Co. Ltd for extracts from *Shakespeare Our Contemporary*, a University Paperback by Jan Kott, translated by Boleslaw Taborski, Copyright © 1964 by Panstwowe Wydawnictwo Naukowe and Copyright © 1965, 1966 by Doubleday & Co, Inc.; Thames and Hudson Ltd for an extract from *The Uses of Enchantment* by Bruno Bettelheim; Random House, Inc., and Brandt & Brandt, Inc., for an extract from *West Side Story* by Laurents and Sondheim.

The publishers and the author would like to thank the following people for permission to reproduce copyright material: Sophie Baker for figs. 11, 16, 19, 39, 41, 42; British Tourist Authority for fig. 38; Nobby Clark for figs. 46, 49; Joe Cocks for figs. 8, 24, 35; Columbia for figs. 9, 10; Connoisseur Films for fig. 13; Zoe Dominic for figs. 12, 18, 30, 47, 48; M.E.P.L. for fig. 45; Robert Harding for figs. 26, 33; Harris Films for fig. 50; Herald Photo Service for fig. 27; Marcel Hodges Photography for fig. 37; Holte Photographics Ltd for figs. 31, 40; Robert Kingston (Films) Ltd for fig. 50; M.G.M. for figs. 14, 15; National Film Archive for figs. 1, 2, 4, 9, 10, 13, 14, 15, 50; National Portrait Gallery for fig. 43; Morris Newcombe for fig. 23; Paramount Pictures for figs. 1, 2; Questors Theatre for fig. 37; Stuart Robinson for fig. 7; Mrs Houston Rogers for figs. 3, 6, 22, 44; Royal Opera House for fig. 7. Figs. 8, 11, 19, 23, 28, 29, 35, 41, 46, 49 reproduced by permission of the Governors of the Royal Shakespeare Theatre, Stratford upon Avon. Shakespeare Birthplace Trust for figs. 25, 32, 34, 36; *Solihull News* for fig. 5; Donald Southern for fig. 20; United Artists for fig. 4; Reg Wilson for fig. 17.

Romeo and Juliet

(in order of appearance)

Michael Aspel	*presenter*
Peter Ustinov	*playwright*
Ian McKellen	*actor*
Hilary Belden	*teacher*
Eileen Atkins	*actress*
Judi Dench	*actress*
Olivia Hussey	*actress*
Anna Calder-Marshall	*actress*

MICHAEL ASPEL:

Romeo and Juliet is the story of two young people who fall in love at first sight and get married the next day in secret. And it does need to be a secret because they come from two families who are involved in a long, complicated and violent feud. Do you remember *West Side Story*? This is the same story except that in the original both lovers are dead by the time the play ends. Before either Romeo or Juliet has appeared on stage, a prologue informs us that they are star-crossed; that's to say their horoscopes aren't too good. What does actor and playwright, Peter Ustinov, think of the story – after all, he borrowed much of it for his comedy, *Romanoff and Juliet*?

PETER USTINOV:

To my mind a tragedy is merely a comedy that's gone wrong, just as a comedy is a tragedy that's gone right. Star-crossed lovers – they're not really star-crossed at all, they're brought to ruin largely by the imbecility of their families. It's too easy to say that they're star-crossed. My point in setting them in embassies is that embassies are a sort of artificial family in which such disasters can still take place.

MICHAEL ASPEL:

Shakespeare's Romeo and Juliet certainly have a disastrous time in late medieval Italy in Verona.

IAN MCKELLEN:

I wonder whether, as you read *Romeo and Juliet*, you think that it couldn't happen today, that people just don't behave in the way that the Montagues and the Capulets do. But consider this –

> Two households, both alike in dignity
> In fair Belfast, where we lay our scene,
> From ancient grudge break to new mutiny,
> Where civil blood makes civil hands unclean.
> From forth the fatal loins of these two foes
> A pair of star-crossed lovers take their life;
> Whose misadventured piteous overthrows
> Doth with their death bury their parents' strife.
>
> (Prologue)

I mean, is it conceivable that two lovers in the middle of Belfast, one Catholic, one Protestant, could begin to solve the terrible problems of that city and that community, as Shakespeare suggests two lovers solved very similar problems in Verona? It would be a very brave man who would present *Romeo and Juliet* on the stage in Belfast at the moment in the terms I've been suggesting. I think it would cause riots. That's how relevant I think *Romeo and Juliet*, one of Shakespeare's most artificial plays, could be to modern life.

MICHAEL ASPEL:

Belfast instead of Verona. It might sound a little strange. But there is actually often a modern-day parallel to be found and that is what we're looking for. We're placing set books in a contemporary context, and we're going to have a close look at *Romeo and Juliet* in great detail. Hilary Belden helps us to explore the structure of the play and shows how it is built around three fights. Remember how quickly everything happens. The lovers meet on Sunday, they marry on Monday, and they're dead by dawn on

Thursday. That sounds almost comic, but the speed of the events is important if you're going to think about the play as a tragedy and ask who is responsible for it. We've been having a look through some old O-Level papers and it does look as though you'll need to think about this, so look for suggestions about who's to blame. Is it fate, or chance, or perhaps just the feud? Maybe the older generation are out of touch? Are the lovers themselves irresponsible?

HILARY BELDEN:

As far as I can see, *Romeo and Juliet* is really the story of an impossible love affair. It starts with an almost empty stage and it starts on a calm day in Verona. There are the two servants from one household and they are simply talking to each other. And then, very suddenly and very quickly, their conversation becomes a fight as soon as they see two servants from the other of the two main households in Verona. The fight explodes almost immediately. You can think of the play as one where there are three tremendous fights. In the first one, which begins the play, nobody gets killed. We turn away from that fight to a very quiet scene, with Romeo, and then another quiet scene with Juliet. Romeo is the son of the house of the Montagues. He's infatuated with a girl called Rosaline. He's not interested in the feud; all he's interested in is Rosaline herself.

MICHAEL ASPEL:

Well, that's a red herring in a play called *Romeo and Juliet*.

EILEEN ATKINS:

Who else would start, when you know it's going to be the greatest love story in the world, with Romeo being in love with another girl? I mean, it's brilliant, because it's absolutely true.

HILARY BELDEN:

Juliet, on the other hand, is not quite fourteen and she has never been in love and she is not concerned about being in love. And when her mother starts to talk to her, just after this fight, about marriage, she says, 'It is an honour that I dream not of.'

MICHAEL ASPEL:

She does later on, and there's where our three Juliets come in. First of all, Judi Dench who played Juliet in 1960 in Franco Zeffirelli's stage production.

JUDI DENCH:

It's said in the theatre that you can't play Juliet until you look too old to play it. It's always been produced so that she's rather statuesque and speaks the verse very beautifully, and you have to have a lot of experience to do that. Well, Zeffirelli cut across that by having John Stride and myself looking very young indeed. For instance, the nightie that I wore was a child's nightie he had copied from one he'd seen in Verona.

MICHAEL ASPEL:

I wonder whether Zeffirelli used that again when he directed his later film of *Romeo and Juliet*? Olivia Hussey played Juliet and she was only fifteen at the time. Zeffirelli wanted to know what Olivia Hussey thought Juliet looked like.

OLIVIA HUSSEY:

He said, 'What is your perfect image of Juliet?' And I said, 'Well, long, blonde hair and blue eyes and a dreamy look.' And he said, 'Ah, you don't know anything.' I had a feeling for Juliet. It was dramatic, and it was something that was a great release for me.

MICHAEL ASPEL:

Our third Juliet is Anna Calder-Marshall. She and Ian McKellen played the two lovers in a radio production.

ANNA CALDER-MARSHALL:

I think that what is fascinating about Juliet is that in the course of the play you see her mature from a child to a woman. She's incredible to play because in the beginning she's so young and slightly silly and gorgeous with the Nurse. They laugh their heads off at the Nurse's bawdy jokes.

MICHAEL ASPEL:

There are plenty of lovely, bawdy jokes to counteract the drama. You can try and spot them, if you like, when you're rereading the opening scenes and the scenes where Mercutio appears. Not always obvious, these jokes. But back to our hero.

HILARY BELDEN:

Romeo, who is desperately unhappy about the girl he's in love with, wants to find a way of seeing her again. And, quite by chance or possibly by fate, he discovers that she will be at a party that very same evening. He goes to the party and there he sees another very beautiful girl.

MICHAEL ASPEL:

It was love at first sight. Romeo and the girl declare their love for one another, just like that. Obviously they found a quiet corner, far away from the rest of the party. They only discover afterwards that he's Romeo and a Montague, and she's Juliet and a Capulet from the other side of the feud. So Romeo and Juliet leave the dance convinced of their undying love for one another. They meet later that night in the garden of Juliet's home, they confirm their passion, and they arrange to marry the next day. This, of course, is the famous balcony scene, the one that's become a theatrical cliché and is always, by the way, being mis-quoted, like so much of Shakespeare. But Ian McKellen has been doing some detective work.

IAN MCKELLEN:

Never take anything for granted in Shakespeare. Always try and discover it for yourself. I'll give you a good example of that. I was playing Romeo in *Romeo and Juliet* in London at the Aldwych Theatre, and at the back of the stalls you can't see the balcony. And of course there has to be a balcony in *Romeo and Juliet*. Does

there? Where in the play is a balcony ever mentioned? Nowhere,
is the answer to that. Why in the balcony scene is Juliet on a
balcony? Because it's tradition, not because Shakespeare asked
for it. Because if you put Juliet on a balcony at the back of the
stage in an Elizabethan theatre, that means Romeo, in looking at
Juliet, has to have his back to the audience. And how can he
speak all those lines for the audience's benefit if he's got his back
to them? I think that Romeo and Juliet in that scene should be on
the same level; they should be able to touch; they should be able
to run into each other's arms; they should be able to make love;
and the point about the scene is that they don't. Juliet is restricted
by the pressures she feels from her father's morality and his
politics. And she is frightened – she is constantly talking about
fear. She's frightened of the dark, she's frightened of the guards
in the grounds, she is frightened of the dogs. And she says, 'Not
today. Tomorrow. Let's get married first.'

JUDI DENCH:

Juliet thinks, 'I'm never going to see him again. Maybe he's
saying things now, maybe he's had a drink of wine too much and
he's just saying it. He belongs to a family that my family don't
talk to.' And then, suddenly, in the middle of the night, he is in
the garden, and he's actually able to speak to her. I can't believe
that anybody who has ever felt any degree of love wouldn't
understand what Juliet is trying to say. When, for instance, in
the balcony scene she says:

> Thou knowest the mask of night is on my face,
> Else would a maiden blush bepaint my cheek
> For that which thou hast heard me speak tonight.
> Fain would I dwell on form – fain, fain deny
> What I have spoke. But farewell compliment!
> Dost thou love me?

> (II. 2. 85–90)

He wants to swear by the moon that he will be constant. And she
says, 'O, swear not by the moon, th'inconstant moon.' She
suddenly has a premonition of fear. 'It is too rash, too unadvised,
too sudden;/Too like the lightning, which doth cease to be/Ere

one may say "It lightens."' The terrible feeling: 'It's all happened much too quickly. I'm too frightened to actually put it into words.'

IAN MCKELLEN:

If you put Juliet on a balcony, the reason that Romeo and Juliet don't touch is *because* she is on a balcony. But that's not the real reason at all. The reason is inside Juliet herself and it's in getting rid of that, those pressures which she has been brought up with, that she grows up and becomes, not a little girl any more, but someone worthy to be Romeo's wife. I doubt if there's ever been a production of the play within living memory which hasn't had a balcony but perhaps, in your school, you could do the first production. It would be very exciting indeed to discover why those two characters don't fling themselves into each other's arms at that point.

MICHAEL ASPEL:

Do you think it's worth a try? Shakespeare's always being re-worked. Back to the story. They do get married the next day. Perhaps it will all work out despite Friar Laurence and Juliet's fears that it's all a bit too fast. That afternoon Romeo comes back to Verona.

HILARY BELDEN:

This is the second fight. You need to imagine a very hot day, people wandering about rather bored, nothing to do except pick a fight with the other side. Romeo comes back through the streets of Verona and walks straight into Juliet's cousin, Tybalt. Tybalt is an extremely vicious, violent gang-leader on the Capulet side, and he wants to fight Romeo for one simple reason, which is that when Romeo came to the Capulet party, the party at which he met Juliet, Tybalt saw him, overheard him, realized that he was a Montague, and wanted to fight him, simply for coming to that party, for gatecrashing it. Tybalt meets Romeo and insists that he wants to fight him. Romeo's great friend, Mercutio, is with him on this hot, sultry day, and Mercutio is only too willing to join in a fight with Tybalt.

JUDI DENCH:

They're young people. There's a fight and quite suddenly, before you realize it, Mercutio has actually been hurt. Suddenly there's a death in the street and it's Juliet's cousin.

HILARY BELDEN:

That's the second fight, and it's at that point that you realize, I think, that the love affair has no chance at all. Up to that point it could perhaps have worked out. They might have been able to keep it secret, but they are not able to now.

MICHAEL ASPEL:

Exit Mercutio, who leaves a dying man's curse over the rest of the proceedings – 'A plague a'both your houses!' And from then on, everything starts to go wrong. Romeo rushes off to the man who married them, Friar Laurence. Juliet is at home and she's waiting for Romeo to come to her that night. It's their wedding night, remember. Instead comes the news that Romeo has killed her favourite cousin, Tybalt. How does she react?

HILARY BELDEN:

For one moment she turns against him bitterly, and then she realizes that this is her husband and she must stand by him.

MICHAEL ASPEL:

It's true love, and she needs her Nurse to help her see Romeo one more time. They spend just one night together.

JUDI DENCH:

If you've spent the night with someone you are passionately in love with, and suddenly as dawn breaks they have to leave, you'll understand how Juliet feels.

IAN MCKELLEN:

Juliet says, 'Wilt thou be gone? It is not yet near day./It was the nightingale, and not the lark,/That pierced the fearful hollow of thine ear.' How close to an ear do you have to be for you to be aware that it's hollow, for its hollowness to be the most remarkable thing about it? You have to be about an inch away from it. He was lying on top of her, or she of him; they were in each other's arms, they were making love. 'The fearful hollow of thine ear.' What does it mean – fearful? He gave a little jump. The hollowness gave a jump. She was so close to him. 'Pierced the fearful hollow of thine ear.' Pierced by the sound that had come from outside, right into the bedroom, through the four-poster bed, under the sheets, into that ear. There isn't a line in Shakespeare, whether it's in an early play like *Romeo and Juliet* or a late play like *Macbeth*, that doesn't merit very, very careful examination to discover exactly what Shakespeare means, because Shakespeare always means something exact.

MICHAEL ASPEL:

Romeo leaves with the dawn. The frightening thing is that Juliet's father is actually planning her marriage to the man of his choice, Count Paris. When Juliet comes downstairs, from having said goodbye to Romeo, she hears of the impending wedding and that makes things a bit difficult. She's married to one man and expected to marry another. Her Nurse, far from helping her, is in favour of the second marriage, and Juliet, remember, can't do what you probably would have, which is walk out on your parents and not come back. So what is she going to do? In the end the only thing she can do is to get Friar Laurence to help. He gives her a potion and she falls asleep. On the morning of her wedding, her family find her, apparently dead.

JUDI DENCH:

No wonder this child goes to the tomb, and will do anything, however frightened she is. She's locked in and she knows that all her ancestors have been buried there. What a terrifying experience.

HILARY BELDEN:

Juliet is put to lie there. Romeo, by this time, has fled. Friar
Laurence sends a message to Romeo, saying, 'Please come back,
Juliet's all right.' But of course the news that Romeo gets is not
that news, that message never reaches him; he simply hears that
she is dead. And the third fight is the one that happens between
Romeo, when he comes riding back to Verona at the dead of night
to see Juliet for the last time, and Paris, who is mourning at her
tomb. I think it's at that moment that you realize how totally
secret this love affair has been because Paris, who was about to be
married to Juliet, cannot understand what Romeo, who is a
Montague, is doing outside the Capulet tomb late at night. Paris
is killed. Romeo goes in to see Juliet and, as he sees her, he is
overwhelmed with her beauty.

IAN MCKELLEN:

> ROMEO
> . . . How oft when men are at the point of death
> Have they been merry! which their keepers call
> A lightning before death. O how may I
> Call this a lightning? O my love, my wife!
> Death, that hath sucked the honey of thy breath,
> Hath had no power yet upon thy beauty.
>
> (V. 3. 88–93)

That's a sexy image, isn't it? Sucking the honey of thy breath.
Death, as a person, sucks the honey of thy breath. That's a
metaphor, an image of tongues – of tasting, of being very close,
being inside each other.

> Shall I believe
> That unsubstantial death is amorous,
> And that the lean abhorred monster keeps
> Thee here in dark to be his paramour?
> For fear of that I still will stay with thee
> And never from this palace of dim night
> Depart again. Here, here will I remain
> With worms that are thy chambermaids.
>
> (V. 3. 102–9)

That's a little joke but it's a black joke, isn't it? Where do those worms crawl in the dead body and in what sense are they chambermaids? They're in and out of the folds of her dress. They are in and out of the folds of her flesh, into her mouth, into her nose, into her ears – all the places that a lover's tongue can go, those worms are crawling. And then he looks at the phial of poison.

HILARY BELDEN:

Then he kills himself. She wakes up. She sees his dead body lying there and kills herself. And it's at that point, when the noise of the fight and everything else has aroused the watch, the police force, that everybody else comes running and realizes what this feud has finally cost them. All the young people, in fact, are dead – Mercutio, Tybalt, Romeo and Juliet.

MICHAEL ASPEL:

It's a tragic situation. Everyone you like is dead. Some you hardly know are dead. Even Romeo's mother has died of grief at her son's banishment. So who are you going to blame for all this? Can you blame anyone? After all, it's chance that Romeo gatecrashes a Capulet party and meets Juliet. It's chance that stops Friar Laurence's message from reaching Romeo. But that can't be all. Surely Shakespeare must have intended us to think that fate is involved; star-crossed lovers they're called. And there is another mention of stars. When Romeo is about to drink the poison, he says he will 'shake the yoke of inauspicious stars'; he's had enough of his ill-fated life. No one will ever agree whose fault it all is, that's the interesting thing. You could blame Juliet's parents – although they don't know about Romeo, they do know she's very upset about Tybalt and in no mood for a wedding. Perhaps they push her into pretending to be dead, which then really happens. And some people blame Romeo and Juliet themselves. They're certainly in a hurry. *You* have to make up your mind about this tragedy and who is to blame, you have to go back to the play and collect your evidence. Don't be frightened of all those exam questions that ask: 'If Juliet's parents had treated her with more sympathy, the tragedy would never have happened.

How far do you consider this a true statement?' You're only being asked what you think. What does Anna Calder-Marshall think about this old favourite from the examiners: 'Discuss the view that the downfall of Romeo and Juliet is the result of their own immaturity.'?

ANNA CALDER-MARSHALL;

If that's immaturity, I don't mind, I call it maturity, because they loved. I may be over-romantic or place too much importance on love, but I do think that it governs a great deal of life. I think it's terribly important. They were in the most terrible dilemma. If they had decided that because they were Montagues and Capulets they should remain apart, just because in the past they were meant to be enemies, I think that would have been immaturity, the immaturity of their parents. Their parents learned by their children's desire to be together.

IAN MCKELLEN:

Romeo and Juliet is the most famous love story of all time because it constantly makes sense. It's the story of two lovers trapped in a society which is alien to them, which is against them. It's the story of youth versus age, love versus hate, life versus death. It isn't that Romeo and Juliet are poor little lovable creatures who are surrounded by a monstrous society. I think the society is the norm. I think the middle-aged people, the parents, the Tybalts, behave as most people behave. We are always ready to hate the foreigner. The extraordinary people in the play are Romeo and Juliet. They are not just a couple in love. They are extraordinarily in love. They somehow know that they are star-crossed, in the sense that they are going to die. Their passion is so great that it cannot be contained. Now that may all sound airy and fairy, but when you're in love yourself you know what it's like to be Romeo and Juliet.

Shakespeare's source

Shakespeare took the story of Romeo and Juliet from a long poem: *The Tragicall History of Romeus and Juliet* by Arthur Brooke. (The story itself had been told several times before Brooke wrote his poem.) Shakespeare followed Brooke's version closely, though he made important changes in it, as he nearly always did when he was following a source. The main change was in the time scheme. In Brooke's poem the story takes place over several months; in Shakespeare's play the story takes only four days. A modern critic describes the effect of this compression:

A straightforward temporal pressure is exerted in *Romeo and Juliet*, in which Shakespeare displays his early skill. Arthur Brooke's *Tragical History* dealt in a leisurely narrative covering nine months; Shakespeare's play has its lovers assaulted by time, and its audience with them. Three days are all that Romeo and Juliet are granted, while Juliet's father jocularly fires her suitor's ardours:

CAPULET ... bid her – mark you me ? – on Wednesday next –
But soft! what day is this ?
PARIS   Monday, my lord.
CAPULET Monday! Ha, ha! Well, Wednesday is too soon.
A' Thursday let it be. A' Thursday, tell her,
She shall be married to this noble earl.

(III. 4. 17–21)

Subject to a grim irony, a confident daughter asks her father's pardon, only to find that he lops off a further precious day, one which proves fatal:

Send for the County. Go tell him of this.
I'll have this knot knit up tomorrow morning.

(IV. 2. 23–4)

Shakespeare continues to press the point with repeated reminders: 'we'll to church tomorrow' – 'prepare him up/Against tomorrow', while the Friar vainly tries to warn Romeo in time. Chance will blast the fortunes of the lovers, although time has been tightening the net since the Prince banished Romeo in III, 1. It seems not a moment

before the wedding morning is upon them, and old Capulet bustles in
to rouse the family with

> Come, stir, stir, stir! The second cock hath crowed.
>
> (IV. 4. 3)

until the stage is alive with the servants of an excited household. All
this in twenty minutes' playing time.

(J. L. Styan, *Shakespeare's Stagecraft*, Cambridge
University Press, 1967)

You can construct an actual timetable of the events in the play
quite easily. The play opens on a Sunday morning with the street
brawl, the Capulets' ball is on Sunday night, Romeo and Juliet
marry on Monday afternoon and their tragic wedding night is on
Monday night, on Tuesday night Juliet takes Friar Laurence's
potion, her funeral is on Wednesday, and on Wednesday night
Romeo returns from Mantua and the lovers die in Juliet's tomb.
The play ends at daybreak on Thursday.

The nights are as crowded with incident as the days. In the
Capulet household, nobody seems to get much sleep. Quite
apart from the young lovers, there is a constant bustle of activity,
what with the ball, Capulet's late-night dinner with Paris, and
the preparations for Juliet's wedding. The nights are short, the
afternoons are long, and the whole play seems full of the atmosphere of a hot Mediterranean summer.

Brooke's poem was strongly moralistic and its message was
quite different from that of Shakespeare's play. In his preface
Brooke wrote:

And to this end, good Reader, is this tragical matter written, to describe
unto thee a couple of unfortunate lovers, thralling themselves to unhonest desire; neglecting the authority and advice of parents and
friends; conferring their principal counsels with drunken gossips and
superstitious friars; attempting all adventures of peril for the attaining
of their wicked lust, using auricular confession, the key of whoredom
and treason, for furtherance of their purpose, abusing the honourable
name of lawful marriage to cloak the shame of stolen contracts; finally
by all means of unhonest life hasting to most unhappy death.

So Brooke stresses the disobedience of the young lovers and their blindness to everything except their own wild desires. But Shakespeare makes us feel that Romeo and Juliet's passion is magnificent, and that their feelings are finer than those of ordinary people. Shakespeare does make fun of one kind of love in the play, Romeo's unhappy and poetic love for Rosaline. That is shown as a conventional hopeless love affair in which a lover sighs for his cruel mistress, who refuses to listen to his pleas. Nothing could be further from the overwhelming frankness of Romeo and Juliet's passion:

> O gentle Romeo,
> If thou dost love, pronounce it faithfully.
> Or if thou thinkest I am too quickly won,
> I'll frown, and be perverse, and say thee nay,
> So thou wilt woo. But else, not for the world.
> (II. 2. 93–7)
> My bounty is as boundless as the sea,
> My love as deep. The more I give to thee,
> The more I have, for both are infinite.
> (II. 2. 133–5)

A pair of star-crossed lovers

Before *Romeo and Juliet* begins we are told in the Prologue that the lovers are victims of misfortune, and that their love will end in death. Much of the poignancy that we feel when we watch the early scenes between Romeo and Juliet comes from our being made constantly aware of the doomed nature of their love.

Fortune is a major force in the play. The tragedy is unavoidable; it advances steadily. But the events that precipitate it are the products of chance – the misfortune of Tybalt's fight with Mercutio, the pure accident by which Friar Laurence's letter fails to reach Romeo.

Both Romeo and Juliet have premonitions of the tragedy that awaits them. Before Romeo even goes into the Capulets' house he has a feeling that he is on the threshold of a fatal event.

> Some consequence, yet hanging in the stars,
> Shall bitterly begin his fearful date
> With this night's revels . . .
>
> (I. 4. 107-9)

While Juliet, looking down on Romeo from her window after their night together, has a sudden and prophetic vision of him:

> O God, I have an ill-divining soul!
> Methinks I see thee, now thou art so low,
> As one dead in the bottom of a tomb.
>
> (III. 5. 54-6)

The references to fate, chance and fortune build up throughout the play.

Is the sheer ill luck of Romeo and Juliet a sign that a total and passionate love like theirs is always doomed in this world, or that it somehow *seeks* a tragic conclusion? Friar Laurence's cautious fears about the lovers' feelings are perhaps proved true by the plot:

> These violent delights have violent ends,
> And in their triumph die, like fire and powder,
> Which as they kiss consume.
>
> (II. 6. 9-11)

Is fortune a neutral force in the play, or is the lovers' death a judgement on their love? However brief and doomed it is, it still blazes gloriously – 'like the lightning, which doth cease to be/ Ere one may say "It lightens."'

Italy

Virtue once made that country mistress over all the world. Vice now maketh that country slave to them that before were glad to serve it . . . For sin, by lust and vanity, hath and doth breed up everywhere common contempt of God's word, private contention in many families, open factions in every city . . .

The Elizabethans had a fairly lurid picture of the Italians. Italians were intensely stylish – courtiers followed their fashions and copied their manners – but they were also thought of as corrupt and decadent, quarrelsome, revengeful and devious. The most celebrated Italian political writer of the century, Niccolò Machiavelli, was so feared and hated that his name became part of the English language and was used to describe the sort of wicked scheming that the Elizabethans thought was the hallmark of Italian politics. It was customary for young lords to travel to Italy as part of their education, in order to polish their court manners and to visit the home of the ancient Romans, but there was growing doubt as to whether this was a suitable way for a young man to spend his time.

Italy, the Paradise of the earth, and the Epicure's heaven, how doth it form our young master? . . . From thence he brings the art of atheism, the art of epicurizing, the art of whoring, the art of Sodomitry.

Italian books were often translated into English. Shakespeare took several of the plots of his plays from Italian sources. The English view of the Italians may have owed something to these romances, which were full of intrigue, disguise, murder and passion – the usual ingredients of popular literature. Many people thought that Italian literature was corrupt and that it would subvert religion and morals and undermine the English way of life.

Ten sermons at Paul's Cross do not so much good for moving men to true doctrine, as one of those books do harm with enticing men to ill living. Yea, I say farther, those books tend not so much to corrupt honest living, as they do to subvert true religion.

The Italians were thought of as hot-tempered Latins, always spoiling for a fight. They had developed the art of duelling – in *Romeo and Juliet* Mercutio makes fun of fashionable Italian fighting styles and duelling jargon. They were a by-word for feuding, for taking sides and for bearing grudges. In 1593 Nashe wrote:

I have heard of a box on the ear that hath been revenged thirty years after.

We still have national stereotypes today, and some of them have not changed all that much. The reserved British still feel the same kind of mixture of fascination and disapproval for the passionate Italians that they did in Elizabethan England. The southern Italians and the Sicilians are still famous for their fierce sense of family honour – the Mafia originated in Sicily. And Italy still has a big reputation for Latin lovers.

Juliet's Nurse

In a romantic play, the character of the Nurse strikes an unexpected note of humour and realism. Harley Granville-Barker examines this appealing character:

The Nurse, whatever her age, is a triumphant and complete achievement. She stands foursquare, and lives and breathes in her own right from the moment she appears, from that very first

> Now, by my maidenhead at twelve year old,
> I bade her come.
>
> (I. 3. 2–3)

Shakespeare has had her pent up in his imagination; and out she gushes. He will give us nothing completer till he gives us Falstaff. We mark his confident, delighted knowledge of her by the prompt digression into which he lets her launch; the story may wait. It is not a set piece of fireworks such as Mercutio will touch off in honour of Queen Mab. The matter of it flows spontaneously into verse, the phrases are hers and hers alone, character unfolds with each phrase. You may, indeed, take any sentence the Nurse speaks throughout the play, and only she could speak it. Moreover, it will have no trace of the convention to which Shakespeare himself is still tied (into which he forces, to some extent, every other character), unless we find her burlesquing it. But the good Angelica – which we at last discover to be her perfect name – needs no critical expanding, she expounds herself on all occasions; nor explanation, for she is plain as daylight; nor analysis, lest it lead to excuse; and she stays blissfully unregenerate. No one can fail to act her well that can speak her lines. Yet they are so supercharged with life that they will accommodate the larger acting – which is the revelation of a personality in terms of a part – and to the full; and it may be as rich a personality as can be found. She is in everything

1, 2. Romeo's fight with Tybalt – two stills from the Zeffirelli film.

3. *'Tell me, daughter Juliet, how stands your disposition to be married?'* The Zeffirelli production at the Old Vic in 1960.

4. *Balcony scene,* West Side Story *version.*

5. *Francesca Annis as Juliet and Ian McKellen as Romeo in a recent Royal Shakespeare Company production.*

6, 7. *Two scenes from the final act of the* Romeo *and* Juliet *ballet. Romeo (Nureyev) finds the 'dead' Juliet, and Juliet, waking, discovers the corpse-strewn crypt. Royal Opera House, 1965.*

inevitable; from her 'My fan, Peter' when she means to play the discreet lady with those gay young sparks, to that all unexpected

> Faith, here it is.
> Romeo is banished; and all the world to nothing
> That he dares ne'er come back to challenge you.
> Or if he do, it needs must be by stealth.
> Then, since the case so stands as now it doth,
> I think it best you married with the County.
>
> (III. 5. 213–18)

– horrifyingly unexpected to Juliet; but to us, the moment she has said it, the inevitable thing for her to say.

This last turn, that seems so casually made, is the stroke that completes the character. Till now we have taken her – the 'good, sweet Nurse' – just as casually, amused by each comicality as it came; for so we do take the folk that amuse us. But with this everything about her falls into perspective, her funniments, her endearments, her grossness, her good nature; upon the instant, they all find their places in the finished picture. And for a last enrichment, candidly welling from the lewd soul of her, comes

> O, he's a lovely gentleman!
> Romeo's a dishclout to him. An eagle, madam,
> Hath not so green, so quick, so fair an eye
> As Paris hath. Beshrew my very heart,
> I think you are happy in this second match,
> For it excels your first; or if it did not,
> Your first is dead – or 'twere as good he were
> As living here and you no use of him.
>
> (III. 5. 219–26)

Weigh the effect made upon Juliet, fresh from the sacrament of love and the bitterness of parting, by the last fifteen words of that.

> Speak'st thou from thy heart?
>   And from my soul too,
> Or else beshrew them both.
>   Amen!

It is gathered into the full-fraught 'Amen'. But best of all, perhaps, is the old bawd's utter unconsciousness of having said anything out of the way. And when she finds her lamb, her ladybird, returning from shrift with merry look – too merry – how should she suppose she has not given her the wholesomest advice in the world?

We see her obliviously bustling through the night's preparations for this new wedding. We hear her – incredibly! – start to wake Juliet from her sleep with the same coarse wit that had served to deepen the girl's blushes for Romeo's coming near. We leave her blubbering grotesquely over the body she had been happy to deliver to a baser martyrdom. Shakespeare lets her pass from the play without comment. Is any needed?

(Harley Granville-Barker, *Complete Prefaces to Shakespeare*, Batsford, 1972)

West Side Story

Romeo and Juliet is a story that several writers and composers have reworked; it has become a ballet, an orchestral suite, a musical. In 1956 Jerome Robbins took the story, set it among the tenements of the West side of New York City, and made *West Side Story*. In the musical, the Capulets and Montagues are replaced by two street gangs, the Jets and the Sharks. The Jets are white Americans, the Sharks are Puerto Ricans. Tony, from the Jets, falls in love with Maria, the sister of Bernardo, the leader of the Sharks. In this scene the lovers, who have just met at a dance, manage to snatch a few minutes together when Tony climbs up the fire escape to Maria's flat. This is, in fact, the balcony scene . . .

11.00 p.m. A back alley.
   A suggestion of buildings; a fire escape climbing to the rear window of an unseen flat.
   As Tony sings, he looks for where Maria lives, wishing for her. And she does appear, at the window above him, which opens on to the fire escape. Music stays beneath most of the scene.

TONY[*sings*] Maria, Maria . . .
MARIA Ssh!
TONY Maria!!
MARIA Quiet!
TONY Come down.
MARIA No.

TONY Maria . . .

MARIA Please. If Bernardo –

MAN'S VOICE [*offstage*] Maruca!

MARIA Wait for me!

   [*She goes inside as the buildings begin to come back into place.*]

TONY [*sings*] Tonight, tonight,

  It all began tonight,

  I saw you and the world went away.

MARIA [*returning*] I cannot stay. Go quickly!

TONY I'm not afraid.

MARIA They are strict with me. Please.

TONY He's at the dance. Come down.

MARIA He will soon bring Anita home.

TONY Just for a minute.

MARIA [*smiles*] A minute is not enough.

TONY [*smiles*] For an hour, then.

MARIA I cannot.

TONY Forever!

MARIA Ssh!

TONY Then I'm coming up.

WOMAN'S VOICE [*from the offstage apartment*] Maria!

MARIA *Momentito*, Mama . . .

TONY [*climbing up*] Maria, Maria –

MARIA *Callate!* [*Reaching her hand out to stop him*] Ssh!

TONY [*grabbing her hand*] Ssh!

MARIA It is dangerous.

TONY I'm *not* 'one of them'.

MARIA You are; but to me, you are not. Just as I am one of them –

   [*She gestures towards the apartment.*]

TONY To me, you are all the –

   [*She covers his mouth with her hand.*]

MAN'S VOICE [*from the unseen apartment*] Maruca!

MARIA *Si, ya vengo, Papa.*

TONY Maruca?

MARIA His pet name for me.

TONY I like him. He will like me.

MARIA No. He is like Bernardo: afraid. [*Suddenly laughing*] Imagine being afraid of you!

TONY You see?

MARIA [*touching his face*] I see you.

TONY See only me.

MARIA [*sings*] Only you, you're the only thing I'll see forever.
  In my eyes, in my words and in everything I do,
  Nothing else but you
  Ever!

TONY And there's nothing for me but Maria,
  Every sight that I see is Maria.

MARIA Tony, Tony . . .

TONY Always you, every thought I'll ever know,
  Everywhere I go, you'll be.

MARIA All the world is only you and me!
    [*And now the buildings, the world fade away, leaving them suspended
  in space.*]
  Tonight, tonight,
  It all began tonight,
  I saw you and the world went away.
  Tonight, tonight,
  There's only you tonight,
  What you are, what you do, what you say.

TONY Today, all day I had the feeling
  A miracle would happen –
  I know now I was right.
  For here you are
  And what was just a world is a star
  Tonight!

BOTH Tonight, tonight,
  The world is full of light,
  With suns and moons all over the place.
  Tonight, tonight,
  The world is wild and bright,
  Going mad, shooting sparks into space.
  Today the world was just an address,
  A place for me to live in,
  No better than all right,
  But here you are
  And what was just a world is a star
  Tonight!

                    (Laurents and Sondheim, *West Side Story*
                          (1959), Heinemann, 1972)

Macbeth

MICHAEL ASPEL:

Travel back in time to a barbaric, eleventh-century Scotland, a smoking world of battles, unbridled ambition and black magic. Macbeth is our man and one with quite a track record. His fortunes were the misfortunes of Scotland. This play is not one for the squeamish. There's a chorus line of corpses and cackling hags. You can certainly count *Macbeth* among Shakespeare's blackest tragedies. Shakespeare dwells on darkness throughout this play. It is an evil force but it's also the mask of night beneath which Macbeth achieves his diabolic destiny. Over the last four hundred years, the play has cast its doleful spell not only upon Macbeth but over the actors themselves. There are some terrible tales, tales of retracting daggers that don't retract on the night. And many is the witch whose cackle has turned to a curse as she's caught her shins on a cauldron. In fact, many actors won't even mention the title of the play, so it's not surprising that in the theatre superstitions surround any production of *Macbeth*. When Roman Polanski made it into a film, the man he chose to play the lead was Jon Finch, who survived to set the scene.

JON FINCH:

It's called the unmentionable. You're not allowed to say 'Macbeth' in a theatre or in a dressing room. If you even quote from the play, you have to go outside the dressing room, turn round three times, whistle, spit or something like that. Ken Tynan's theory is that it's an unlucky play because most of it is performed in the dark and on battlements, and people tend to fall off battlements when they can't see the edges of the rostrum or whatever. I looked both ways crossing a one-way street while I was making the picture and, in fact, the only accident we had is where my finger got split down the middle during a sword fight.

MICHAEL ASPEL:

Macbeth is known as the Scottish play and it was written with a Scottish audience in mind, because watching the first performance was King James I, who was also James VI of Scotland. The play tells the story of Scotland's survival in the days of clan warfare. Here's Ian McKellen.

IAN MCKELLEN:

I've seen productions of *Macbeth* where all the cast spoke with Scottish accents, where they wore kilts, where they had bagpipes, where the witches did a sort of threesome reel, and that didn't help the play at all because I don't think Shakespeare's play depends upon it being set in Scotland. It could be set in Wales, America, anywhere in the world. It's about people in a political emotional situation.

TIMOTHY WEST:

It's always attracted me, I think right from the very first Shakespeare I ever read, as the most compulsive play. I find the imagery, the darkness and mysticism of the play absolutely engrossing. The difficulties, of course, are the difficulties of why, why it happens.

IAN MCKELLEN:

Of course, he's a brave and famous warrior, a sort of mixture of Muhammed Ali and Moshe Dayan in one. He's the man who saved Scotland at the beginning of the play – he was the great golden boy, there was nothing that he couldn't achieve, he was everybody's favourite. He tried to control fate with the aid and encouragement of the witches, who seemed themselves to have some control over fate.

MICHAEL ASPEL:

Don't forget that at the start of the play our golden boy has won the Scottish war and beaten the Norwegians. Macbeth is on his way up. King Duncan is favouring him with new titles and even the spirits know about his success story.

WITCHES:

> All hail, Macbeth! Hail to thee, Thane of Glamis!
> All hail, Macbeth! Hail to thee, Thane of Cawdor!
> All hail, Macbeth, that shalt be king hereafter!
>
> (I. 3. 47–9)

MARTIN AMIS:

It's often said that the witches merely put the idea in Macbeth's head and that's all they need to do, but I think it's deeper than that. Very early on Macbeth says, 'So foul and fair a day I have not seen,' immediately picking up the language of the witches before he's even come across them. The language is always, in Shakespeare, the clue. If you can find consistent imagery in a Shakespearean play, you always know it's telling you something, and the imagery of *Macbeth* certainly would suggest that the witches are actual evil forces who can bring these things about.

MICHAEL ASPEL:

Martin's right to emphasize the patterns of imagery in *Macbeth*. They are the best evidence of Shakespeare's intentions. It's a topsy-turvy world where man's ambition is shown to be a primal force that can easily become a poison. Macbeth wrestles with the

terrible temptation of killing a king to become a king himself.
Here's Patricia Hayes, who has played the First Witch.

PATRICIA HAYES:

In our first production at Stratford, we descended. We went up
in the black-out on a huge metal ring – the three of us had to get
on in the pitch dark – and it whisked us up, right up high, and
then it slowly descended and hovered and, while we were coming
down, a curious noise – a sort of humming noise – started and
out of that we spoke. I thoroughly enjoyed playing that wicked
old woman with all her schemes. We decided, among ourselves,
that the witches believed to some extent in the powers of their
magic and their spells, but that really they were charlatans. They
were camp followers, they found out little titbits of gossip, they
knew the sort of man that Macbeth was, and they used the fact
that he was rather weak to work on him. And obviously he was in
rather a hysterical state coming from battle; between Lady
Macbeth and the witches he hadn't really got a chance.

MICHAEL ASPEL:

You might well have a chance to answer something like this
favourite foul question from past papers: 'Is *Macbeth* a tragedy
of ambition or witchcraft?' Well, one thing's for sure, the witches
alone couldn't work the wicked wonders. An equally strong lure
comes from Lady Macbeth who, to Eileen Atkins, appears not
to be such a lady.

EILEEN ATKINS:

I just don't feel that Lady Macbeth is a woman. Now I know
Shakespeare wrote his parts for boys, but he's written the most
wonderful womanly characters, and I don't understand Lady
Macbeth. I think it was one time when he just got too much into
thinking of a male mind, I don't know whether the boy playing
it was a favourite or something, or maybe he was attempting to
show us a very male mind in a woman. But you know, it's always
done with this monster coming on stage, and you think, 'I don't
know anybody who would quite do that.' She seems so vicious.

There's lovely Lady Macduff with her little pretty chickens, the children, and you think 'I understand *her*'; but I always want to know where are Mrs Macbeth's children. If we see Mrs Macduff's children, why don't we see Mrs Macbeth's?

MICHAEL ASPEL:

Well, that's an interesting thought but one which Judi Dench, our Lady Macbeth, wants to argue about.

JUDI DENCH:

What Shakespeare intended was not at all a strong, imperious, rather frightening lady to come walking on – I think he needs a very feminine person to come on, who actually has a great passion for her husband and is tremendously ambitious for him. If you have a very strong, certain person playing the part who looks very sure, and rather frightening, why on earth does Shakespeare then give her a speech invoking spirits, in a kind of black mass, to give her strength to carry out what she believes is going to get her husband a smashing job – that is to be King?

EILEEN ATKINS:

If you were very ambitious and if you used that nervousness for striving at the beginning – she knows just what she wants, and she's going to get it, even if she has to do it through her husband. There have been women who have been behind men, and in fact you know that they're the stronger of the two.

JUDI DENCH:

She actually asks the spirits to take away her sexuality. She's got the letter from Macbeth saying that he met the three witches, and that they have promised him that he's going to become King of Scotland. Because of the passion that I think she feels for him, she wants him to have the best possible thing that is offered to him. Therefore suddenly, when the servant comes in and says, 'The King comes here tonight,' she is completely taken off guard. And then, knowing that the time is actually going to run out now, she invokes the spirits; she has to turn to some supernatural thing. She says, 'Come, you spirits/That tend on mortal thoughts, unsex me here/And fill me from the crown to the toe top-full/Of direst cruelty.' She actually asks to be made cruel.

MICHAEL ASPEL:

And it's at this stage that we realize how much more there is to this plot than just evil spirits. Psychology is mixed in with the psychic forces which work upon Macbeth, and his dreams and his aspirations are not unfamiliar ones.

JOHN COX:

We can all be Macbeth. We aren't human if we haven't at some time succumbed to temptation, if we haven't made the wrong choice, so I think there's a very strong personal identity in *Macbeth* which we can share. Similarly, when he comes under the manipulative control of Lady Macbeth with those strong, unnaturally strong, speeches she makes, we too know what it's like to be influenced by another person. Now all this makes for a play in which there's an extraordinary construction.

TIMOTHY WEST:

People tend to think of the play in terms of its two sorts of effects. They say, 'How can this man be a soldier and a poet? How can he, if he has this sensitive, poetic soul, do this appalling deed?'

MICHAEL ASPEL:

Those 'How cans' are compatible as long as Macbeth keeps his conscience, and it's this which comes to haunt him out on the battlements of his castle. 'Is this a dagger which I see before me,/The handle toward my hand? ... Or art thou but/A dagger of the mind, a false creation,/Proceeding from the heat-oppressèd brain?' Well, this feverish hallucination doesn't stop Macbeth from murdering Duncan, and after Duncan's death when Macbeth becomes King of Scotland he progressively becomes harder. He refuses to take stock of his actions because 'To know my deed 'twere best not know myself.' Macbeth opts for moral blindness throughout the second half of the play. That sensitive, poetic side of him becomes concentrated into strong attacks against his future victims. Banquo, the friend and fellow soldier who had happened to be with Macbeth that day when the witches first spoke out, tops the death list. Public enemy number two is the noble Lord Macduff, whose refusal of an invitation to dinner at court triggers off Macbeth's hatred. Macbeth becomes a new and a terrible man. Chris Burge is interested in Macbeth's language of loathing. For example, this is hardly a fond thought for your best friend, Banquo: Macbeth says he is 'But sickly in his life, which in his death were perfect.'

CHRIS BURGE:

The strong point is that what he says in fact mirrors the morality of the play. All the good characters use images, use language, which reflects a basic moral pattern of good and evil, of order and disorder, of sleep and insomnia, of medicine and of disease. Macbeth uses these images too, but he never seems to realize just what he has done – that he has killed a king.

JUDI DENCH:

Having driven him through to the murder of Duncan, Lady Macbeth then thinks – now they have become King and Queen – that is going to be it for the rest of their lives. What she doesn't understand is that, having tasted blood, Macbeth goes on to want to kill more, to remove more people from his way. She doesn't see that anything further has got to be done; she thinks she's achieved what is right for them both.

TIMOTHY WEST:

Macbeth has sent Banquo, who he's already beginning to suspect knows the truth, away, and has actually told one of the murderers to go and kill him. Lady Macbeth, whose resolve is waning as Macbeth's ambition grows, comes on discontented, aimless, and sees Macbeth in a deep gloom. And he says, 'O, full of scorpions is my mind, dear wife!/Thou know'st that Banquo and his Fleance lives.' She replies, 'But in them nature's copy's not eterne', meaning they don't go on for ever, and she's referring of course to the thing he's told her about Banquo begetting kings where he can't. And he says:

> There's comfort yet! They are assailable.
> Then be thou jocund. Ere the bat hath flown
> His cloistered flight, ere to black Hecat's summons
> The shard-borne beetle, with his drowsy hums,
> Hath rung night's yawning peal, there shall be done
> A deed of dreadful note.
>
> . . . .
>
> Be innocent of the knowledge, dearest chuck,
> Till thou applaud the deed. Come, seeling night,
> Scarf up the tender eye of pitiful day,
> And with thy bloody and invisible hand,
> Cancel and tear to pieces that great bond
> Which keeps me pale. Light thickens
> And the crow makes wing to the rooky wood;
> Good things of day begin to droop and drowse,
> Whiles night's black agents to their preys do rouse.
> Thou marvell'st at my words; but hold thee still.
> Things bad begun make strong themselves by ill.
> So, prithee, go with me.
>
> (III. 2. 39–56)

JUDI DENCH:

And then suddenly, having had that little bit of glory of being crowned, when they're King and Queen, the rift between them starts to broaden and you hear that he doesn't spend any time with her. He cuts her off, and gradually of course they go different ways – he going on to do further deeds, and she pulling back because she can't go with him.

MICHAEL ASPEL:

Of all the ghastly deeds which Macbeth goes on to do, none is more dreadful than the murder of Lady Macduff and her children. The news of this foul slaughter of his fair family reaches Macduff in England, where he's gone to raise an army against Macbeth.

Meanwhile, back in Scotland, Macbeth believes himself invulnerable because he's paid a second visit to the three weird sisters who have told him so.

WITCHES:

> Round about the cauldron go;
> In the poisoned entrails throw:
> Toad that under cold stone
> Days and nights has thirty-one.
> Sweltered venom, sleeping got,
> Boil thou first i'the charmèd pot.
> Double, double, toil and trouble;
> Fire burn, and cauldron bubble.
>
> (IV. i. 4–11)

MICHAEL ASPEL:

From that cauldron they conjured up three spirits, each with its message to Macbeth. He must 'beware Macduff' and yet 'Be bloody, bold, and resolute; laugh to scorn/The power of man; for none of woman born/Shall harm Macbeth.' And finally he learns that 'Macbeth shall never vanquished be, until/Great Birnam Wood to high Dunsinane Hill/Shall come against him.' Well, those prophecies sound like a firm insurance policy for immortality, but never forget that it was the witches who said, 'Security is mortal's chiefest enemy.'

JOHN COX:

There's a lot of talk about the play's supernatural qualities and I think sometimes the wrong emphasis is put on it, because frequently in Shakespeare the supernatural is there for atmospheric background. That is why the imagery in *Macbeth*, particularly of darkness and obscurity and the sinister aspects of night time, is so strongly brought out. It's background, it's atmosphere. All right, we've got apparitions, phenomena, omens, cackling figures and so on, but there's nothing in *Macbeth* which is more frightening than Macbeth's own actions, Macbeth's own mind.

MICHAEL ASPEL:

Remember that this is the mind that once thought, 'I dare do all that may become a man;/Who dares do more is none.' So, by his own definition, Macbeth has been deflected from man's proper dominions to become the monster of the last scenes – yelling at the few servants that remain faithful, safe in his mad belief that he's protected by prophecy. Even as he thinks he sits secure in great Dunsinane Castle, Birnam Wood is on the move, and camouflaged behind its branches are the advancing armies of Malcolm and Macduff. Approach Macbeth, Ian McKellen.

IAN MCKELLEN:

So there he is alone – his friends are leaving him, now his wife has left him. And the messenger comes in to say, 'The queen, my lord, is dead.' And Macbeth says:

> She should have died hereafter.
> There would have been a time for such a word –
> Tomorrow, and tomorrow, and tomorrow,
> Creeps in this petty pace from day to day
> To the last syllable of recorded time;
> And all our yesterdays have lighted fools
> The way to dusty death. Out, out, brief candle!
> Life's but a walking shadow, a poor player
> That struts and frets his hour upon the stage
> And then is heard no more. It is a tale
> Told by an idiot, full of sound and fury,
> Signifying nothing.
>
> (V. 5. 17–28)

'Life's but a walking shadow'. A walking shadow – what does that mean? Well, it's a shadow following a man walking along a country lane lit in the dark by a guttering candle. It's a shadow which hardly exists – it's wavering about the road. All the evidence is that Shakespeare was not just a playwright but also an actor. There is a phrase in the theatre, not used now very much but which was quite common in the last century – 'a walking gentleman'. A walking gentleman was an actor who played any old part. Life isn't even a walking gentleman, he's a walking shadow.

8. 'Stay, you imperfect speakers! Tell me more!' Macbeth (Ian McKellen) questions the witches. Royal Shakespeare Company, The Other Place, 1973.
9. The witches in Roman Polanski's film.

Two versions of the banquet scene :   10. *A still from the film* Joe Macbeth.

11. *Macbeth (Nicol Williamson) and Lady Macbeth (Helen Mirren) welcome their guests. Royal Shakespeare Company, Aldwych, 1975.*

2. 'What, will the line stretch out to the crack of doom?' The vision of Banquo's escendants as kings of Scotland. National Theatre Company, 1972.

13. Macbeth and Lady Macbeth in the Japanese film Throne of Blood.

'Life's but a walking shadow, a poor player/That struts and frets his hour upon the stage/And then is heard no more.' What happens to an actor when he is off the stage? When there is no audience – he's finished, he's nothing. If you can understand that then you can begin to understand what Macbeth feels like when he says that the whole of his life is as meaningless as me standing up on this stage now talking to you. And Macbeth's conclusion is that: 'It is a tale/Told by an idiot, full of sound and fury,/ Signifying nothing.'

MICHAEL ASPEL:

And Macbeth's own tale is speeding now to its close. He deserves to die and he wants to die. He no longer believes in omens which are revealed to him now as semantic shams, just playing with words, a few branches being called Birnam Wood. And a man born by caesarean section can break the spell that held Macbeth secure, but 'none of woman born/Shall harm Macbeth'. The man who was 'from his mother's womb/Untimely ripped' is the one person Macbeth feared all along. The witches had warned him to 'beware Macduff!' Macbeth dies bravely at Macduff's hand. Death for a man whose life had become meaningless was merciful, and at Macbeth's end you feel pity, for this man might have been a hero. But his only epitaph is 'this dead butcher'. But Shakespeare's tragic vision transcends our readiness to hand out blame, and instead he brings us to an understanding of the self-torture and the self-waste of Macbeth. And, as your moment of high drama draws near, here are Helen Mirren, Judi Dench and Ian McKellen. Is this an exam paper they see before them?

HELEN MIRREN:

I'm looking at a question here: '"This dead butcher and his fiend-like queen" – how far is this an adequate description of either Macbeth or Lady Macbeth?' I would say that it's an adequate description of Macbeth or Lady Macbeth as far as the character who is saying it is concerned. I'm sure that neither Lady Macbeth nor Macbeth themselves would agree with this description; they both have very rational and sensible reasons for what they do, otherwise they wouldn't do it. They are not born fiends and I think this is Shakespeare's message in writing a play like *Macbeth* – you don't look at these characters as mad killers from the beginning, somehow separate from the rest of humanity. They are ordinary people like you or I. They just have one flaw in their character.

JUDI DENCH:

As far as fiend-like is concerned, she is indeed fiend-like. She asks spirits to give her this kind of power in order to be able to do the one deed, killing Duncan, that she wants. But after that she starts to back away – one murder is bad enough. At the beginning it's not a King and Queen of Scotland or even great people, it's people who you can recognize. Anyone who is driven to the extremes of greed or passion or lust or ambition can go this way. There but for the grace of God can go anybody. We don't tell a great epic, tragic story; we try and tell a psychological story about people.

IAN MCKELLEN:

There could not be a more black statement of what life is like at its very worst. Shakespeare's not recommending that we should feel like that all the time, but he is saying that, until you've known the depth of the blackness of life, you perhaps won't be able to appreciate the joy and the light which so much of his other plays express.

James I

For the first time, under King James, Shakespeare's company became the official royal theatre company, 'The King's Men'. *Macbeth* was certainly a play which should have pleased King James, and it's more than likely that the first performance of it was given at the court.

The plot was taken from Holinshed's *Chronicles*, like the plots of all of Shakespeare's History plays. Perhaps, having shown the triumphant accession of the Tudors in his earlier plays, Shakespeare decided to write a play with a setting in Scottish history partly as a compliment to the King, who was the first of the new Stuart line of kings. Although it deals with a lot of the same ideas as the History plays, *Macbeth* is always thought of as a Tragedy, not as a History. It is Macbeth's crime, his guilt, and his inner world which are at the centre of the play. He kills Duncan with his own hands in Shakespeare's play; this most important murder is physical and bloody, not a cold political act by hired assassins.

This is also a play *about* Scotland and about the Scottish monarchy. King James could trace his ancestry back to Fleance, son of Banquo. The 'cauldron' scene, where Macbeth sees the apparitions of Banquo and his descendants, would have had a particular significance for the play's first audience:

MACBETH
Thou art too like the spirit of Banquo. Down!
Thy crown does sear mine eye-balls. And thy hair,
Thou other gold-bound brow, is like the first.
A third is like the former. – Filthy hags,
Why do you show me this ? – A fourth ? Start, eyes!
What, will the line stretch out to the crack of doom ?
Another yet ? A seventh ? I'll see no more!
And yet the eighth appears, who bears a glass
Which shows me many more. And some I see

That two-fold balls and treble sceptres carry.
Horrible sight! . . .

(IV. I. III–21)

James I of England was also James VI of Scotland. The two-fold balls are probably the orbs of the two countries (James had been crowned twice, at Scone and at Westminster), and the treble sceptres represent the two used in the English coronation ceremony and the one used in the Scottish ceremony. So here is King James actually appearing, pictured in the magic glass, on the stage.

The story of the witches is also one in which the King would have taken a considerable interest. He had written a book called *Daemonologie* in 1597. This was a treatise on witchcraft, which James, like many intellectuals and theologians of the time, saw as the worst kind of heresy, a form of devil-worship. Soon after he came to the throne an act increasing the penalties against witchcraft was passed by Parliament, and in the years that followed a great many witches were condemned and burnt.

Finally, this play about the murder of a good king was bound to have a topical appeal. In 1605 the Gunpowder Plot had been discovered. If it had succeeded, King James, the members of the House of Lords and of the House of Commons would all have been blown to pieces by the Roman Catholic conspirators. Shakespeare probably shared the general horror that had been felt at the idea of such a bloodbath.

James I and the divine right of kings

The Tudor monarchs had made the doctrine of the divine right of kings an important part of their political philosophy. Though the actual political strength of the crown was gradually declining as the balance of power in the country shifted to Parliament, the Tudors still maintained the mystical belief that the King drew his authority directly from God. James I, Elizabeth's successor, upheld this belief very strongly. In 1609, in a speech to Parliament, he said:

Kings are not only God's Lieutenants on earth and sit upon God's throne, but even by God himself they are called gods.

He was impatient of the growing power of Parliament. In 1614 he observed to the Spanish ambassador:

I am surprised that my ancestors should ever have permitted such an institution to come into existence. I am a stranger, and found it here when I arrived so that I am obliged to put up with what I could not get rid of.

James was a studious and thoughtful man. He occupied himself with the political and intellectual questions of his day, and published several books on such matters. In 1598, while he was James VI of Scotland, but not yet James I of England, he had written a book called *The True Law of Free Monarchies*, in which he set out his ideas about kingship. He took the doctrine of divine right seriously, even literally, and saw no real reason why royal power should be limited by laws or parliaments. He did, however, grant that it could sometimes be justifiable to depose a tyrant:

. . . a Tyrant's miserable and infamous life, armeth in the end his own Subjects to become his burreaux [executioners]: and although that rebellion be ever unlawful on their part, yet is the world so wearied of him that his fall is little meaned by the rest of his subjects, and but smiled at by his neighbours.

Which is not a bad description of the mood of the last act of *Macbeth*.

The doctrine of the Tudors had also contained this fail-safe clause. There were two cases in which it was considered legitimate to kill a king:

(a) when the king was a tyrant, so bad that he was completely corrupted; or

(b) when the king had himself attacked a previous king and taken the crown by force.

In all other circumstances, however, men were duty bound to obey the king:

Whatsoever man, woman, or child is by the consent of the whole realm established in the royal seat, *so it have not been injuriously procured by rigour of sword and open force*, but quietly by title whether of inheritance, succession, lawful bequest, common consent or election, is undoubtedly chosen by God to be his deputy.

So, according to all the accepted rules, Malcolm and Macduff were well within their rights in rebelling against King Macbeth, who had murdered his way to the throne and gone on safeguarding his tyranny by more murders. But Macbeth's original murder of Duncan broke all the rules. He himself recognized the complete absence of any grounds for an attack on Duncan, who had been a good and respected king:

> Besides, this Duncan
> Hath borne his faculties so meek, hath been
> So clear in his great office, that his virtues
> Will plead like angels, trumpet-tongued, against
> The deep damnation of his taking-off;
>
> (I. 7. 16–20)

Like the holy king of England who is described later in the play, Duncan really does seem divinely appointed. The fate that awaits his usurper is therefore, in terms of the doctrine of divine right, inevitable.

Shakespeare's sources

For his plays about Scottish history, Shakespeare drew heavily on the main source for his English History plays, Holinshed's *Chronicles*. Here is an extract that shows the importance of the *Chronicles* as a source for *Macbeth*.

It fortuned as Makbeth and Banquho iournied towards Fores, where the king then laie, they went sporting by the waie togither without other company saue onelie themselues, passing thorough the woods and fields, when suddenlie in the middest of a laund, there met them three women in strange and wild apparell, resembling creatures of elder world, whome when they attentiuelie beheld, woondering much at the sight, the first of them spake and said: All haile Makbeth, thane of Glammis (for he had latelie entered into that dignitie and office by the death of his father Sinell). The second of them said: Haile Makbeth thane of Cawder. But the third said: All haile Makbeth that heereafter shalt be king of Scotland.

Then Banquho: What manner of women (saith he) are you, that seeme so little fauourable vnto me, whereas to my fellow heere, besides high offices, ye assigne also the kingdome, appointing foorth nothing for me at all? Yes, (saith the first of them) we promise greater benefits vnto thee, than vnto him, for he shall reigne in deed, but with an vnluckie end: neither shall he leaue anie issue behind him to succeed in his place, where contrarilie thou in deed shalt not reigne at all, but of thee those shall be borne which shall gouern the Scotish kingdome by long order of continuall descent. Herewith the foresaid women vanished immediatlie out of their sight. This was reputed at the first but some vaine fantasticall illusion by Mackbeth and Banquho, insomuch that Banquho would call Mackbeth in iest, king of Scotland; and Mackbeth againe would call him in sport likewise, the father of manie kings. But afterwards the common opinion was, that these women were either the weird sisters, that is (as ye would say) the goddesses of destinie, or else some nymphs or feiries, indued with knowledge of prophesie by their necromanticall science, bicause euerie thing came to passe as they had spoken. For shortlie after, the thane of Cawder being condemned at Fores of treason against the king committed; his lands, liuings, and offices were giuen of the kings liberalitie to Macbeth.

The same night after, at supper, Banquho iested with him and said: Now Mackbeth thou hast obteined those things which the two former sisters prophesied, there remaineth onelie for thee to purchase that which the third said should come to passe. Wherevpon Mackbeth reuoluing the thing in his mind, began euen then to deuise how he might atteine to the kingdome; but yet he thought with himselfe that he must tarie a time, which should aduance him thereto (by the diuine prouidence) as it had come to passe in his former preferment. But shortlie after it chanced that king Duncane hauing two sonnes by his wife which was the daughter of Siward earle of Northumberland, he made the elder of them called Malcolme prince of Cumberland, as it were thereby to appoint him his successor in the kingdome, immediatlie after his deceasse. Mackbeth sore troubled herewith, for that he saw by this his hope sore hindered (where, by the old lawes of the realme, the ordnance was, that if he that should succeed were not of able age to take the charge vpon himselfe, he that was next of bloud vnto him should be admitted) he began to take counsell how he might vsurpe the kingdome by force, hauing a just quarrell so to doo (as he tooke the matter) for that Duncane did what in him lay to defraud him of all manner of title and claime, which he might in time to come, pretend vnto the crowne.

The woords of the three sisters also (of whom before ye haue heard) greatlie incouraged him herevnto, but speciallie his wife lay sore vpon him to attempt the thing, as she that was verie ambitious, burning in vnquenchable desire to beare the name of a queene. At length therefore, communicating his purposed intent with his trustie friends, amongst whome Banquho was the chiefest, vpon confidence of their promised aid, he slue the king at Enuerns, or (as some say) at Botgosuane, in the sixt yeare of his reigne. Then hauing a companie about him of such as he had made priuie to his enterprise, he caused himselfe to be proclaimed king, and foorthwith went vnto Scone, where (by common consent) he receiued the inuesture of the kingdome according to the accustomed maner.

King James attends a witch's trial

In about 1590, when King James was king of Scotland, but not yet king of England, he attended the trial of a woman who was accused of being a witch, called Agnes Sampson:

. . . The said Agnes Sampson was after brought again before the King's Majesty and his Council, and being examined of the meetings and detestable dealings of those witches, she confessed that upon the night of All-hallow Even last, she was accompanied, as well with the persons aforesaid, as also with a great many other witches, to the number of two hundred, and that all they together went to sea, each one in a riddle or sieve, and went into the same very substantially, with flagons of wine, making merry and drinking by the way in the same riddles or sieves, to the kirk of North Berwick in Lothian; and that after they had landed, took hands on the land, and danced this reel or short dance, singing all with one voice,

> Commer go ye before, commer go ye,
> Gif ye will not go before, commer let me.

At which time she confessed, that this Geillis Duncane did go before them, playing this reel or dance, upon a small trump, called a Jew's trump, until they entered into the kirk of North Berwick.

These confessions made the King in a wonderful admiration, and he sent for the said Geillus Duncane, who upon the like trump did play the said dance before the King's Majesty, who in respect of the strangeness of these matters, took great delight to be present at their examinations.

The said Agnes Sampson confessed that the devil, being then at North Berwick kirk attending their coming, in the habit or likeness of a man, and seeing that they tarried over long, he at their coming enjoined them all to a penance, which was, that they should kiss his buttocks, in sign of duty to him; which being put over the pulpit bare, everyone did as he had enjoined them. And having made his ungodly exhortations, wherein he did greatly inveigh against the King of Scotland, he received their oaths for their good and true service towards him, and departed; which done, they returned to sea, and so home again. At which time, the witches demanded of the devil, 'Why he did bear such hatred to the King?' Who answered, 'By reason the King is the greatest enemy he hath in the world.' All which their confessions and depositions are still extant upon record.

The Hecate scenes

When Pepys saw *Macbeth* in 1667 he wrote: 'Though I have seen it often, yet it is one of the best plays for a stage, and variety of dancing and music, that ever I saw.' It's certainly possible to produce *Macbeth* in a lot of different ways – but as a *musical*? Yet that really is what it became, along with many other classic plays, in the seventeenth-century theatre. Spectacle was admired. The witches' scenes were consequently played up, and it seems probable that the scenes with Hecate were written in, to add to the witches' parts and to bring in the song and dance routines that Pepys so much enjoyed. The two songs that Hecate sings obviously were inserted – they also appear in another play, Middleton's *The Witch* – and it's likely that Hecate's dialogue which introduces them was written specially to introduce the songs. Most modern productions leave out Hecate altogether.

Sarah Siddons on Sarah Siddons'
Lady Macbeth (1785)

*(Mrs Siddons, whose performance as Lady Macbeth influenced actresses
for over a century, describes how she approached the part)*

It was my custom to study my characters at night, when all the dom-
estic cares and business of the day were over. On the night preceding
that in which I was to appear in this part for the first time, I shut myself up, as usual, when all the family were retired and commenced my
study of Lady Macbeth. As the character is very short, I thought I
should soon accomplish it. Being then only twenty years of age, I
believed, as many others do believe, that little more was necessary than
to get the words into my head; for the necessity of discrimination, and
the development of character, at that time of my life, had scarcely
entered into my imagination. But, to proceed. I went on with tolerable
composure, in the silence of the night (a night I can never forget), till I
came to the assassination scene, when the horrors of the scene rose to
a degree that made it impossible for me to get farther. I snatched up
my candle, and hurried out of the room, in a paroxysm of terror.

My dress was of silk, and the rustling of it, as I ascended the stairs to
go to bed, seemed to my panic-struck fancy like the movement of a
spectre pursuing me. At last I reached my chamber, where I found my
husband fast asleep. I clapt my candlestick down upon the table, without the power of putting the candle out, and threw myself on my bed,
without daring to stay even to take off my clothes. At peep of day, I
rose to resume my task; but so little did I know of my part when I
appeared in it, at night, that my shame and confusion cured me of
procrastinating my business for the remainder of my life.

About six years afterwards I was called upon to act the same character in London. By this time I had perceived the difficulty of assuming a
personage with whom no one feeling of common general nature was
congenial or assistant. One's own heart could prompt one to express,
with some degree of truth, the sentiments of a mother, a daughter, a
wife, a lover, a sister, etc., but to adopt this character must be an effort
of the judgment alone.

Therefore, it was with the utmost diffidence, nay, terror, that I
undertook it, and with the additional fear of Mrs Pritchard's reputation
in it before my eyes. The dreaded first night at length arrived, when,

just as I had finished my toilette, and was pondering with fearfulness my first appearance in the grand, fiendish part, comes Mr Sheridan, knocking at my door, and insisting, in spite of all my entreaties not to be interrupted at this to me tremendous moment, to be admitted . . .

Well, after much squabbling. I was compelled to admit him, that I might dismiss him the sooner, and compose myself before the play began. But, what was my distress and astonishment when I found that he wanted me, even at this moment of anxiety and terror, to adopt another mode of acting the sleeping scene. He told me he had heard with greatest surprise and concern that I meant to act it without holding the candle in my hand; and, when I urged the impracticability of washing out that 'damned spot' with the vehemence that was certainly implied by both her own words and by those of her gentle-woman, he insisted, that if I did put the candle out of my hand, it would be thought a presumptuous innovation, as Mrs Pritchard had always retained it in hers. My mind, however, was made up, and it was then too late to make me alter it; for I was too agitated to adopt another method. My deference to Mr Sheridan's taste and judgment was, however, so great, that, had he proposed the alteration whilst it was possible for me to change my own plan, I should have yielded to his suggestion; though even then it would have been against my own opinion, and my observation of the accuracy with which somnambulists perform all the acts of waking persons.

The scene, of course, was acted as I had myself conceived it, and the innovation, as Mr Sheridan called it, was received with approbation. Mr Sheridan himself came to me, after the play, and most ingenuously congratulated me on my obstinacy. When he had gone out of the room, I began to undress; and while standing up before my glass, and taking off my mantle, a diverting circumstance occurred to chase away the feelings of this anxious night; for while I was repeating, and endeavouring to call to mind the appropriate tone and action to the following words, 'Here's the smell of blood still!' my dresser innocently exclaimed, 'Dear me, ma'am, how very hysterical you are tonight; I protest and vow, ma'am, it was not blood but rose-pink and water; for I saw the property-man fix it up, with my own eyes.'

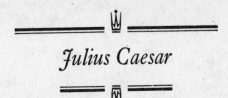

Julius Caesar

(in order of appearance)

Michael Aspel	*presenter*
Sir John Gielgud	*actor*
Sheridan Morley	*critic*
John Schlesinger	*director*
James Mason	*actor*
Patrick Stewart	*actor*
John Cox	*teacher*
Timothy West	*actor*

MICHAEL ASPEL:

It's toga time. We're back in the year 44 B.C. Rome rules the waves and we Britons are slaves, conquered by the mighty Julius Caesar. Caesar was the conquering hero, and soon this general began to talk like a god. But his was a republican Rome – those Hollywood-style Roman emperors were a thing of the future – and Caesar's colleagues in the Senate weren't prepared to put up with the man's presumption. The god would have to go. This is one of Shakespeare's Roman plays, a powerful drama of dictatorship and revolution, and one of the most popular in the Shakespeare canon. And it's not entirely unfamiliar to Sir John Gielgud.

SIR JOHN GIELGUD:

This is a play which I know very well because I have played in it ever so many times. When I was a schoolboy, I played Mark Antony – made rather a sensation, or so I thought at the time, in my little toga at the age of about twelve. Then I went to the Old Vic and I played Mark Antony again. Then I played Cassius at Stratford-upon-Avon and again in the film. And then I played Caesar in another film, and I played Caesar at the National Theatre last year. So I've played all the principal parts, except Brutus.

MICHAEL ASPEL:

Brutus, Cassius and Mark Antony. They are the stars of this story, not Caesar, who's dead for most of it. So if it's not about the man who gives his name to the play, what should we be looking for? Sheridan Morley has been doing a lot of homework recently; what has he spotted in this Shakespeare play?

SHERIDAN MORLEY:

The thing to remember about *Julius Caesar* is that it's a power game. It's a play about power, about the grabbing of power and about what you do once you've got power. It's not really an old-fashioned play, and I don't believe it is necessarily a play that could only take place in Rome with these figures. I believe that Caesar and Brutus and Cassius have counterparts all through modern history.

MICHAEL ASPEL:

Yes, that's why the play works so well in twentieth-century settings. Orson Welles put everyone into black shirts and suddenly Caesar and Mussolini were one and the same man. But our Caesar is Sir John Gielgud.

SIR JOHN GIELGUD:

I didn't find Caesar a very congenial character, I don't think he's very nice. I think he's very cold and very priggish, and talks about himself far too grandly before he's murdered. But, in some curious way, there are one or two lines which are so striking that you do get the feeling that he's a very, very important figure, and it was important to have an actor with a good deal of authority playing him. He's a very hysterical kind of man, really, and I suppose in a way he asks for it.

MICHAEL ASPEL:

And he certainly gets it. But you could see Caesar less as a flawed man and more as a political type. Here's the view of John Schlesinger, who directed the play recently at the National Theatre.

14. Brutus (James Mason) ends his speech, and introduces Mark Antony (Marlon Brando) in the film of Julius Caesar.

15. '*Et tu, Brute?*'

16. '*Beware the Ides of March.*' *St George's Theatre, 1979.*

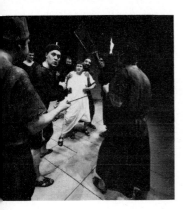

17. 'Tear him to pieces! He's a conspirator.' Cinna the poet is killed by the plebeians. Royal Shakespeare Company, 1972.

18. The petitioners urge Caesar to read their scrolls. Royal Shakespeare Company, 1964.

19. 'Peace, ho! Caesar speaks.' Calpurnia (kneeling), Caesar and Mark Antony. Royal Shakespeare Company, 1973.

JOHN SCHLESINGER:

You can see the character of Julius Caesar either as a demagogue who at all costs had to be removed, or as a dictator in whose footsteps it was very hard to follow. The revolution, in a sense, of the various people that wished to overthrow him went awry, as revolutions often do because the people that take over aren't up to the original character that they've assassinated, or deposed.

MICHAEL ASPEL:

Let's have a look at those assassins. We go back to 15th February 44 B.C., when all Rome is having a party to celebrate Caesar's victory in a civil war against Pompey. It's also the feast of Lupercal and Caesar's great friend, young Mark Antony, is the life and soul of the celebrations. But there are some gloomy faces around town. A soothsayer warns Caesar to 'beware the ides of March'. The date to mark in more modern calendars is 15th March, and it's a red letter day for Cassius, the one with the lean and hungry look. He has plans to kill Caesar then. But first, he wants the support of the noble Brutus. And here's our noble Brutus, James Mason. He's played the part more than once, first when he was twenty-four years old and a bit later in the famous film in 1953.

JAMES MASON:

Brutus is the anchor man of the play. Cassius has the first part, Antony has the middle section and Brutus has the last act. But Brutus is the most important person in the cast, I've always thought, although of course Antony is the most spectacular part. And so I bounded into it rather thoughtlessly and, at the end of it, and even during the process of making the film, I was aware that I was not doing a very good job. Number one, I was juxtaposed with Cassius, John Gielgud.

SIR JOHN GIELGUD:

James Mason, who played Brutus in the film with me, was simply splendid and gave me a certain ambition to play the part myself. But I think that Cassius is the best acting part and I've always thought so because it has the magnificent quarrel scene and the great scene of temptation at the beginning, and the whole attitude of jealousy which everybody can understand – of a jealous, bitter man who finds a dictator a revolting symbol although he admires him in a way. And Cassius is marvellously delineated by Shakespeare as this sour but passionate creature. You can't help but see his point of view.

MICHAEL ASPEL:

Someone who shares it is Patrick Stewart.

PATRICK STEWART:

When I played Cassius at Stratford in 1972 and in London in 1973, the centre of the part for me was two love affairs. Cassius has a love affair with Julius Caesar and a love affair with Brutus, and neither of them are fully consummated. Cassius is an emotional and spontaneous figure in the play, not reflective, not pragmatic in his approach. The very first time we see him, I think he has two tiny speeches and then he talks for three pages about Caesar, who has apparently rejected him. I felt that Cassius' principal longing was to be Caesar's lover, companion, friend. Ideally that's what he would have liked. And because of his rejection, all of his energies are then turned against Caesar, turned towards destroying Caesar.

MICHAEL ASPEL:

It's a potent speech in which Cassius' hurt has turned to hatred. 'Why, man, he doth bestride the narrow world/Like a Colossus, and we petty men/Walk under his huge legs, and peep about/To find ourselves dishonourable graves.' But nothing is more dishonourable, in this play, than the mob. Just like townsfolk in a Western who are baying for the neck of the dishonoured sheriff, one minute they were cheering for Pompey, the next they follow Caesar who 'comes in triumph over Pompey's blood'.

JOHN COX:

I think a very important point to make about *Julius Caesar* is that one is given a privileged position by Shakespeare. We're not only one of the plebeians, one of the crowd, one of the soldiers, but we're the fly on the wall. We are there when, for example, Brutus in soliloquy is feeling his way towards joining the conspirators, working out that rather neat image of Caesar as a serpent's egg.

MICHAEL ASPEL:

While Brutus battles in his mind, Cassius has an instinctive and obsessive awareness that Caesar must die. Cassius and Brutus make an odd couple really and your examiners have got their teeth into this: 'Compare and contrast the principal conspirators.'

TIMOTHY WEST:

Brutus is the nice man, Cassius is the nasty man, but Cassius is always right and Brutus is always wrong. And every time Cassius gives him a piece of advice, if it was acted upon, they'd be in the clear. Brutus says, 'No, no, I don't think we'll do that, I think we'll do so and so,' and is immediately in the soup. Brutus really is the respectable name that you put on the notepaper. If you've got Brutus on your board, you've got a lot of public sympathy and you've got a kind of aura of integrity and respectability.

PATRICK STEWART:

Cassius is a man who needs to have an emotional relationship with somebody all the time, and when one ends he will turn to another one. Perhaps, without being sexist about it, there is a very strong feminine streak in Cassius. He transfers his passion from Caesar to Brutus and that is why he permits himself often to be misguidedly overruled by Brutus, because he is prepared to sacrifice his judgement in order to maintain his emotional relationship with Brutus. And indeed that's what finally destroys him.

MICHAEL ASPEL:

Well, we've considered *Julius Caesar* as a power game. How about in terms of modern-day politics?

JOHN SCHLESINGER:

I was living in America at the time that we were thinking about *Julius Caesar*, and it was impossible not to think a great deal about the production. In fact my original conception of it was to do it all in nice Washington suits. I think that Brutus, who after all is a country gentleman who comes out of retirement and is persuaded to get involved once again in politics, is really rather a sententious character. He's full of so-called moral scruples but in the end, I think, is no better than any of them. He has good intentions. He's certainly always lecturing and moralizing.

JAMES MASON:

Cassius has made the wise suggestion of getting rid of Antony, and Brutus says:

> Our course will seem too bloody, Caius Cassius,
> To cut the head off and then hack the limbs,
> Like wrath in death and envy afterwards;
> For Antony is but a limb of Caesar.
> Let us be sacrificers, but not butchers, Caius.
> We all stand up against the spirit of Caesar,
> And in the spirit of men there is no blood.
> O, that we then could come by Caesar's spirit,
> And not dismember Caesar! But, alas,
> Caesar must bleed for it. And, gentle friends,
> Let's kill him boldly, but not wrathfully;
> Let's carve him as a dish fit for the gods,
> Not hew him as a carcass fit for hounds.
> And let our hearts, as subtle masters do,
> Stir up their servants to an act of rage,
> And after seem to chide 'em. This shall make
> Our purpose necessary, and not envious;
> Which so appearing to the common eyes,
> We shall be called purgers, not murderers.
> And for Mark Antony, think not of him;
> For he can do no more than Caesar's arm
> When Caesar's head is off.

(II. 1. 162–83)

MICHAEL ASPEL:

But that speech shows something worse than a morally sententious man. Brutus made a terrible mistake in allowing Antony to
live. Perhaps the ominous thunderstorm, which raged all night
and gave Caesar's wife such disturbed dreams of disaster, was
also a warning to the conspirators that Brutus was a bungler.
Next morning, against all the signs that were wafting from a
steaming plate of animal entrails, Caesar leaves for the Capitol,
never to return alive. One by one, the conspirators plunge their
daggers into Caesar, who dies with that final discovery of be-
trayal: 'Et tu, Brute?' The date – the ides of March. But, as it
turns out, Caesar isn't the only man who need fear this day. Once
his feeble frame is struck down and that haughty voice silenced,
the spirit of Caesar begins its free, godlike course. His avenging
angels on earth are his nephew, Octavius, and his friend, Mark
Antony, who Brutus so foolishly allowed to live. But there is
worse to follow, because Brutus lets Mark Antony address the
mob after the murder.

JAMES MASON:

You see, Brutus, poor lamb, gets up and makes a very solid,
sensible speech. People cry out, 'The noble Brutus is ascended.
Silence!' and everybody's silent. And Brutus says:

Be patient till the last.
Romans, countrymen, and lovers, hear me for my cause, and be silent,
that you may hear. Believe me for mine honour, and have respect to
mine honour, that you may believe. Censure me in your wisdom, and
awake your senses, that you may the better judge. If there be any in
this assembly, any dear friend of Caesar's, to him I say that Brutus'
love to Caesar was no less than his. If then that friend demand why
Brutus rose against Caesar, this is my answer: not that I loved Caesar
less, but that I loved Rome more . . . Here comes his body, mourned
by Mark Antony, who, though he had no hand in his death, shall receive the benefit of his dying, a place in the commonwealth, as which
of you shall not? With this I depart, that, as I slew my best lover for
the good of Rome, I have the same dagger for myself, when it shall
please my country to need my death.

(III. 2. 12–47)

SIR JOHN GIELGUD:

Mark Antony then addresses the crowd:

> Friends, Romans, countrymen, lend me your ears;
> I come to bury Caesar, not to praise him.
> The evil that men do lives after them,
> The good is oft interred with their bones;
> So let it be with Caesar. The noble Brutus
> Hath told you Caesar was ambitious.
> If it were so, it was a grievous fault,
> And grievously hath Caesar answered it.
> Here, under leave of Brutus and the rest –
> For Brutus is an honourable man;
> So are they all, all honourable men –
> Come I to speak in Caesar's funeral.
> He was my friend, faithful and just to me;
> But Brutus says he was ambitious,
> And Brutus is an honourable man.
> He hath brought many captives home to Rome,
> Whose ransoms did the general coffers fill:
> Did this in Caesar seem ambitious?
> When that the poor have cried, Caesar hath wept;
> Ambition should be made of sterner stuff:
> Yet Brutus says he was ambitious,
> And Brutus is an honourable man.
> You all did see that on the Lupercal
> I thrice presented him a kingly crown,
> Which he did thrice refuse. Was this ambition?
> Yet Brutus says he was ambitious,
> And sure he is an honourable man.
> I speak not to disprove what Brutus spoke,
> But here I am to speak what I do know.
> You all did love him once, not without cause;
> What cause withholds you then to mourn for him?
> O judgement, thou art fled to brutish beasts,
> And men have lost their reason. Bear with me;
> My heart is in the coffin there with Caesar,
> And I must pause till it come back to me.

(III. 2. 74–108)

TIMOTHY WEST:

Antony works on in very much this vein, manipulating the crowd until he gets them into a state to receive what is really his trump card which is to read Caesar's will.

MICHAEL ASPEL:

The mob, enraged by Antony's clever speech, tear through the town leaving in their wake your examiners. 'What,' they ask, 'is the dramatic importance of the crowd?'

SHERIDAN MORLEY:

The crowd, of course, plays a more important part in *Julius Caesar* than in any other Shakespeare play. They are the ones who swing the balance of power from the conspirators towards Mark Antony. They are the ones whom Antony manages to swing, and he swings them because he's a great orator. In the end Antony wins purely on his speech, and the whole of the rest of the play is conditioned by the fact that Antony is very good on a soapbox and neither Brutus nor Cassius are as good as he is in public. So it's a play very much about the crowd. They are the ones whom we first see on the stage at the very beginning of the play – 'Hence! home, you idle creatures, get you home.' They are the characters we see from the first moment of the play right through to the classic 'Friends, Romans, countrymen'. Then they begin to fade out.

JOHN SCHLESINGER:

It's a mob run riot. And the politicians have already started doing worse things than the original dictator has done. Mark Antony and Octavius are already, despite being somewhat opposed to one another, the new authority. And what is the first thing they do? They go through the list of everybody that should be assassinated. You see the mob run riot and say, 'Let's go to so and so's house. Are you a conspirator? Well – he's not a conspirator, but let's kill him anyway.'

TIMOTHY WEST:

I always thought, and every time I see the play I continue to think, that Brutus is a thundering great pompous bore until he gets to Philippi, when we begin to see what the man is really about. It's almost as if Shakespeare wanted there to be two kinds of depersonalized forces of dictatorship and revolution, and that we would judge them for the first half of the play. Then, when these forces actually get onto the battlefield, paradoxically he looks at them as people. And we begin to look at Mark Antony as a rather different sort of person. We think, 'Hello, is he really this marvellous, loyal friend to Caesar, or is he feathering his own nest pretty quickly?' and 'Just who is Octavius Caesar, and surely he's rather sinister?' And Brutus, as I say, begins to reveal an extraordinary nobility.

JOHN COX:

This is what, perhaps, makes the tragedy. We're privileged to be given personal insights, not just seeing the characters, the heroes, the soldiers, the generals, in the public eye. This contrast is what perhaps makes the fullest personal commitment – we can be Caesar and we can be the Fourth Citizen.

MICHAEL ASPEL:

The most striking of these personal insights are those into Brutus and Cassius as they await their fast-approaching fate at the battle of Philippi. On one level their infighting reflects their inability to run anything. Brutus stubbornly insists that his battle plans must be followed although Cassius, as ever, is the better tactician. But beneath this is Brutus' tragic knowledge that his wife has died, and for Cassius there is the final, intense disappointment of the rejected lover. He asks Brutus to 'Strike, as thou didst at Caesar; for I know,/When thou didst hate him worst, thou lovedst him better/Than ever thou lovedst Cassius'. And, as the eagles overhead prophesy both men's doom, Caesar pays Brutus a last visit.

JOHN SCHLESINGER:

Although it's only once in the text you actually see the ghost of Caesar, I deliberately used him several times, multiplying him until in the end he became like any kind of hall or museum where you see the busts of famous men looking down on the action, which in the end essentially is rather petty. I think Brutus at the end is dramatizing his mistakes, and Mark Antony's speech about Brutus finally is one, to me, of some irony.

SHERIDAN MORLEY:

'How far is *Caesar* a play about human weakness?' Of course it is about human weakness, of all kinds of people. First of all, the weakness of Caesar. The weakness of Caesar is his vanity. He will not be put off from going to the Capitol even when he knows, through the dream that his wife has had, that something terrible may happen to him, because he is terrified of seeming a coward. His weakness is his concern about his public image. He doesn't want to be thought cowardly; he doesn't want to be thought afraid; he's not big enough to overcome public feeling about him. Therefore he goes to the Capitol; therefore he is killed. Brutus, again, is a weak man – a man easily dominated by Cassius, a man who at many points in the play can be accused of weakness. Indeed the entire revolution is bungled because of the weakness of Brutus and Cassius, neither of whom have the narrow-minded, powerful determination of Mark Antony. Mark Antony is the only truly powerful character in the play and to that extent the others are different examples of human weakness.

MICHAEL ASPEL:

Shakespeare has left us abundant examples in over nine hundred characters of weakness and strength, love and hate, despair and joy. Within the dry distinctions of tragedies and comedies, History plays and Roman plays, there is a power-house of ideas and images of the politics of co-existence, and the passions and the predicaments of the individual.

JOHN COX:

We're in a century where we don't like moralizing. Shakespeare is not a moralist and I think this is very evident in *Julius Caesar*. He isn't asking us to come to a moral assessment of whether Brutus is right to be idealistic, or whether Antony is wrong to be so unscrupulous in the way he manipulates the Plebeians, for example. He is just observing, and I think this is perhaps his greatest interest. We're not asked to judge, but we are asked to look very closely.

The Elizabethans and the Romans

Shakespeare, like many other Elizabethans, was interested in the world of the ancient Greeks and Romans. In the fifteenth and sixteenth centuries, the artists of Italy and of other European countries were rediscovering the work of classical artists. They based their own sculpture and painting on classical models and revived classical techniques and themes. This revival, or Renaissance, was accompanied by a strong interest in classical literature, history and philosophy. Any educated person read Latin, which was the language of the Church as well as of the Romans, but now the study of Greek became an important part of the curriculum as well. Translations of Greek and Roman writers became enormously popular. A constant stream of translations of classical writings was being published throughout the sixteenth century.

The Elizabethans' particular interest in the Romans may have been a result of the fact that they identified with them in some ways. The Romans had been great travellers and colonizers: their Empire had spread as far as Syria in the East and Britain in the West. (Julius Caesar was, of course, the Roman General who had carried out the conquest of Britain.) In the sixteenth century many nations, but especially England and Spain, were embarking on voyages of trade and conquest, and laying the foundations of new empires to rival that of Imperial Rome.

Also the Elizabethans were becoming a more urban people. Throughout the sixteenth and seventeenth centuries there was a constant population drift to London. The sort of active public life that was developing in sixteenth-century London had parallels in the life of the great metropolis of ancient Rome. Rome was a republic, ruled by a Senate. In Elizabethan England, the power of the Commons was growing, and there was a good deal of curiosity about republican Rome and its system of government. The education of young men was designed to prepare them for active participation in public life. Public speaking was considered a very important art, and law and logic were key subjects. At the same time, public men were expected to be cultured, and physically active. One popular Elizabethan book held up Julius Caesar – soldier, scholar, and statesman – as an example of a thoroughly accomplished man.

Finally, there was a growing interest in *human* matters rather than *religious* matters. The Church had dominated philosophical and intellectual life for centuries. Now there was an upsurge of excitement about the wealth of learning in the works of 'pagan' classical writers. The Romans offered a way of thinking which made this world, not the next, the point of life. They offered new philosophies, like stoicism, which seemed to provide some of the consolations of religion, without its dogma. They were interested in government, in history, and in engineering – in the achievements of men. These interests were echoed by their Elizabethan readers. In time a new word, *humanist*, began to be used. It meant two things: a student of classical literature and philosophy *and* a student of human (rather than religious) affairs.

Shakespeare's source

Shakespeare's source book for *Julius Caesar* was Plutarch's *Lives of the Greeks and Romans*. Plutarch was actually a Greek historian, who was writing about a hundred years after the assassination of Caesar in 44 B.C. In the sixteenth century his book was read widely in Latin, and was also translated into French and English. In fact Sir Thomas North's translation, which Shakespeare obviously used, was a translation from the French translation of Plutarch, not from the original Greek.

In his introduction to the book, Sir Thomas North wrote:

There is no profane study better than Plutarch ... this man, being excellent in wit, in learning and experience, hath chosen the special acts, of the best persons, of the famousest nations of the world.

The Elizabethans enjoyed reading about great men and finding examples in their lives. North's Plutarch was reprinted twice in

Shakespeare's lifetime and continued to sell well until the end of the seventeenth century.

Shakespeare stuck very closely to North's Plutarch in writing *Julius Caesar*. He used three of the Lives – the Life of Brutus, the Life of Caesar, and the Life of Antony. He often took whole passages almost directly out of North. In the *Life of Brutus* one of Lucilius' speeches reads:

I dare assure thee, that no enemy hath taken nor shall take Marcus Brutus alive, and I beseech God keep him from that fortune: for wheresoever he be found, alive or dead, he will be found like himself.

In Shakespeare's play this becomes:

> I dare assure thee that no enemy
> Shall ever take alive the noble Brutus;
> The gods defend him from so great a shame!
> When you do find him, or alive or dead,
> He will be found like Brutus, like himself.
> (V. 4. 21–5)

But Shakespeare was not simply copying North. In the most exciting scene in *Julius Caesar*, the Forum scene, the speeches of Brutus and Antony are entirely Shakespeare's creation. He greatly condensed the time scheme he found in Plutarch and made the events of the plot follow one another much more rapidly. For instance, in Plutarch Antony's funeral speech about Caesar is delivered on the day after Brutus' speech to the people, and Octavius doesn't come to Rome until about six weeks later. In *Julius Caesar* all these things happen in one day and are described within one scene, the Forum scene (III. 2).

This makes a better, more fast-moving plot, and adds to the tension of a play which has been aptly described as 'a political thriller'.

The following extracts from North's version of Plutarch's *Life of Marcus Brutus* describe the assassination of Caesar (III. 1) and Antony's funeral speech (III. 2).

Now all the Senators being entered first into this place or chapter-house where the council should be kept, all the other conspirators straight stood about Caesar's chair, as if they had had something to say unto him. And some say that Cassius, casting his eyes upon Pompey's image, made his prayer unto it, as if it had been alive. Trebonius on the other side drew Antonius aside, as he came into the house where the Senate sat, and held him with a long talk without. When Caesar was come into the house, all the Senate rose to honour him at his coming in. So when he was set, the conspirators flocked about him, and amongst them they presented one Tullius Cimber, who made humble suit for the calling home again of his brother that was banished. They all made as though they were intercessors for him, and took Caesar by the hands, and kissed his head and breast. Caesar at the first simply refused their kindness and entreaties; but afterwards, perceiving they still pressed on him, he violently thrust them from him. Then Cimber with both his hands plucked Caesar's gown over his shoulders, and Casca, that stood behind him, drew his dagger first and strake Caesar upon the shoulder, but gave him no great wound. Caesar, feeling himself hurt, took him straight by the hand he held his dagger in, and cried out in Latin: 'O traitor Casca, what dost thou?' Casca on the other side cried in Greek, and called his brother to help him. So divers running on a heap together to fly upon Caesar, he, looking about him to have fled, saw Brutus with a sword drawn in his hand ready to strike at him: then he let Casca's hand go, and casting his gown over his face, suffered every man to strike at him that would. Then the conspirators thronging one upon another, because every man was desirous to have a cut at him, so many swords and daggers lighting upon one body, one of them hurt another, and among them Brutus caught a blow on his hand, because he would make one in murthering of him, and all the rest also were every man of them bloodied.

Antony's funeral oration

Then Antonius, thinking good his testament should be read openly, and also that his body should be honourably buried, and not in hugger-mugger, lest the people might thereby take occasion to be worse offended if they did otherwise: Cassius stoutly spake against it. But Brutus went with the motion, and agreed unto it; wherein it seemeth he committed a second fault. For the first fault he did, was when he would not consent to his fellow-conspirators, that Antonius should be slain, and therefore he was justly accused, that thereby he had saved and strengthened a strong and grievous enemy of their conspiracy. The second fault was, when he agreed that Caesar's funerals should be as

Antonius would have them, the which indeed marred all. For first of all, when Caesar's testament was openly read among them, whereby it appeared that he bequeathed unto every citizen of Rome 75 drachmas a man; and that he left his gardens and arbours unto the people, which he had on this side of the river Tiber, in the place where now the temple of Fortune is built: the people then loved him, and were marvellous sorry for him. Afterwards, when Caesar's body was brought into the market-place, Antonius making his funeral oration in praise of the dead, according to the ancient custom of Rome, and perceiving that his words moved the common people to compassion, he framed his eloquence to make their hearts yearn the more; and taking Caesar's gown all bloody in his hand, he laid it open to the sight of them all, shewing what a number of cuts and holes it had upon it. Therewithal the people fell presently into such a rage and mutiny, that there was no more order kept amongst the common people. For some of them cried out, 'Kill the murtherers': others plucked up forms, tables, and stalls about the market-place, as they had done before at the funerals of Clodius, and having laid them all on a heap together, they set them on fire, and thereupon did put the body of Caesar, and burnt it in the midst of the most holy places. And furthermore, when the fire was throughly kindled, some here, some there, took burning firebrands, and ran with them to the murtherers' houses that killed him, to set them on fire. Howbeit the conspirators, foreseeing the danger before, had wisely provided for themselves and fled.

Stoicism in *Julius Caesar*

Stoicism was the Roman philosophy that held particular attractions for Elizabethan readers. It was a philosophy of the 'stiff upper lip'. The stoical man could endure hardships, setbacks, even the prospect of death itself, by cultivating a sort of emotional detachment. In a world ruled by chance, the stoic endured whatever fate decreed, and tried to meet either pain or pleasure indifferently. He followed reason, not passion. The Elizabethans found this a manly, tough-minded sort of attitude to life, and Socrates, who was a sort of patron saint of stoicism, became one of their classical heroes. The modern equivalent would be to admire people for their 'cool'.

In an age when violence and death were common and when a lot of accepted ideas were beginning to crumble, perhaps there was a particular need for a philosophy of this kind to hang on to; it offered some kind of formula for meeting life's difficulties. T. S. Eliot said that 'Stoicism is a refuge for the individual in an indifferent or hostile world too big for him', or in other words a way of 'cheering oneself up'.

In *Julius Caesar* Shakespeare's Romans are frequently shown adopting a stoic approach to misfortune. Caesar and Brutus, in particular, try to meet life coolly, but Shakespeare often reveals their inner conflict and indecision. When Caesar's wife begs him not to go to the Capitol because of the terrible omens of the night, he withstands her like a stoic, saying:

> Cowards die many times before their deaths;
> The valiant never taste of death but once.
> Of all the wonders that I yet have heard,
> It seems to me most strange that men should fear,
> Seeing that death, a necessary end,
> Will come when it will come.

(II. 2. 32–7)

But all the same, he changes his mind twice after this apparently final decision. In the assassination scene, when the conspirators crowd round Caesar begging him to pardon Publius Cimber (as a cover for getting close enough to stab him), Caesar's refusal to be moved by the petitioning is a stoical position, but hardly a likeable one:

> I could be well moved, if I were as you;
> If I could pray to move, prayers would move me;
> But I am constant as the northern star,
> Of whose true-fixed and resting quality
> There is no fellow in the firmament.

(III. 1. 58–62)

His final lofty dismissal of Cinna ('Hence! Wilt thou lift up Olympus?') is characteristic of the arrogance that marks these last speeches.

Brutus is also determined to be unshakeable in his resolutions,

20. 'I know a bank where the wild thyme blows.' A scene from the Royal Opera Company production of Benjamin Britten's opera.

21. *Bottom among the fairies, pictured by the eighteenth-century artist, Fuseli.*

22. *'Scratch my head, Peaseblossom.' Royal Opera Company.*

23. *Bottom and the other Athenian workmen begin their rehearsals. Peter Brook's Royal Shakespeare Company production. World Tour, 1972.*

24. *A model of the set of the Brook 'Dream', showing the wire 'trees', the trapezes, Titania's feathery bower, and the cat walk.*

25. *The bower scene from Peter Brook's production at the Royal Shakespeare Theatre in 1970.*

and is sometimes intolerably self-righteous. In the quarrel scene with Cassius he is impassive when he is faced with Cassius' rage and emotion:

> There is no terror, Cassius, in your threats;
> For I am armed so strong in honesty
> That they pass by me as the idle wind,
> Which I respect not.
>
> (IV. 3. 66–9)

But the next half of the scene has presented editors and producers with a lot of problems. Did Shakespeare really write the scene as we have it? Did Brutus, who as we know from his conversation with Cassius has already heard of Portia's suicide, pretend to Messala that he knew nothing about it? Both parts of the scene show Brutus taking up a stoic attitude to Portia's death. To Cassius he says, of himself, 'No man bears sorrow better', and when he has described the circumstances of her suicide he continues, 'Speak no more of her.' To Messala he says that he has heard *no* news of Portia and, being told that she is dead, he comments:

> We must die, Messala.
> With meditating that she must die once,
> I have the patience to endure it now.
>
> (IV. 3. 188–90)

Most editors have suggested that this double revelation is a mistake; that Shakespeare wrote the scene in two ways but did not mean both to appear in the final version. They don't accept that Brutus could have been so hypocritical as to pretend to Messala that he was ignorant of Portia's death. It would make Brutus look as if he was trying to impress Messala with his stoical indifference to misfortune. Messala *is* impressed: 'Even so great men great losses should endure,' he murmurs. Are the editors right in giving Brutus the benefit of the doubt, or is Shakespeare showing us the unacceptable face of stoicism?

Faced with the prospect of his *own* death, Brutus is far from decisive. When Cassius asks him, before Philippi, what he intends to do if they lose the battle, Brutus gives a classic stoic reply, rejecting the idea of suicide as a way of escaping the life of a captive:

> I know not how,
>   But I do find it cowardly and vile,
>   For fear of what might fall, so to prevent
>   The time of life . . .

(V. 1. 102–5)

But when the battle is clearly lost and Cassius has killed himself, Brutus vacillates. He asks first one officer and then another to assist him in committing suicide in the Roman fashion, and finally manages to persuade Strato to hold his sword. He dies just in time to avoid capture. Neither Caesar nor Brutus is the unwavering figure that they aim to be. All along Shakespeare seems to be pointing out that it's easy to strike stoic attitudes, but harder to sustain them when faced with the complexities of real life situations.

The turning point of the play

R. G. Moulton, a Victorian critic, describes the part of the play when the conspirators' moment of triumph is interrupted, and a shadow falls over their success, the shadow of Mark Antony:

The assassination is accomplished, the cause of the conspirators is won: pity notwithstanding we are swept along with the current of their enthusiasm; and the justification that has been steadily rising from the commencement reaches its climax as, their adversaries dispersing in terror, the conspirators dip their hands in their victim's blood, and make their triumphant appeal to the whole world and all time.

CASSIUS Stoop then, and wash. How many ages hence
   Shall this our lofty scene be acted over,
   In states unborn, and accents yet unknown!
BRUTUS How many times shall Caesar bleed in sport,
   That now on Pompey's basis lies along,
   No worthier than the dust!
CASSIUS   So oft as that shall be,
   So often shall the knot of us be called
   The men that gave their country liberty.

(III. 1. 111–18)

Enter a servant: this simple stage-direction is the 'catastrophe', the turning-round of the whole action; the arch has reached its apex and the Reaction has begun. So instantaneous is the change, that though it is only the servant of Antony who speaks, yet the first words of his message ring with the peculiar tone of subtly-poised sentences which are inseparably associated with Antony's eloquence; it is like the first announcement of that which is to be a final theme in music, and from this point this tone dominates the scene to the very end.

> Thus he bade me say:
> Brutus is noble, wise, valiant, and honest;
> Caesar was mighty, bold, royal, and loving:
> Say I love Brutus, and I honour him;
> Say I feared Caesar, honoured him, and loved him.
> If Brutus will vouchsafe that Antony
> May safely come to him, and be resolved
> How Caesar hath deserved to lie in death,
> Mark Antony shall not love Caesar dead
> So well as Brutus living.

> (III. i. 125–34)

In the whole Shakespearean Drama there is nowhere such a swift swinging round of a dramatic action as is here marked by this sudden up-springing of the suppressed individuality in Antony's character, hitherto so colourless that he has been spared by the conspirators as a mere limb of Caesar. The tone of exultant triumph in the conspirators has in an instant given place to Cassius's 'misgivings' as Brutus grants Antony an audience; and when Antony enters, Brutus's first words to him fall into the form of apology. The quick subtlety of Antony's intellect has grasped the whole situation, and with irresistible force he slowly feels his way towards using the conspirators' aid for crushing themselves and avenging their victim. The bewilderment of the conspirators in the presence of this unlooked-for force is seen in Cassius's unavailing attempt to bring Antony to the point, as to what compact he will make with them. Antony, on the contrary reads his men with such nicety that he can indulge himself in sailing close to the wind, and grasps fervently the hands of the assassins while he pours out a flood of bitter grief over the corpse. It is not hypocrisy, nor a trick to gain time, this conciliation of his enemies. Steeped in the political spirit of the age, Antony knows, as no other man, the mob which governs Rome, and is conscious of the mighty engine he possesses in his oratory to sway that mob in what direction he pleases.

(R. G. Moulton, *Shakespeare as a Dramatic Artist*, 1888)

Brutus the political idealist

How can an idealist like Brutus be capable of an act of terrorism? Edward Dowden suggests that Brutus' principles and logic lead him inexorably towards the murder of Caesar:

Brutus is in his orchard alone. He has stolen away from Portia; he is seeking to master himself in solitude, and bring under the subjection of a clear idea and a definite resolve the tumultuary powers of his nature, which have been roused and thrown into disorder by the suggestions of Cassius. In the soliloquy of Brutus, after he has been left alone, will be found an excellent example of the peculiar brooding or dwelling style which Shakspere appropriated at this period to the soliloquies of men. The soliloquies of his women are conceived in a different manner. Of this speech Coleridge has said, 'I do not at present see into Shakspere's motive, his *rationale*, or in what point of view he meant Brutus' character to appear.' Shakspere's motive is not far to seek. He wishes to show upon what grounds the political idealist acts. Brutus resolves that Caesar shall die by his hand as the conclusion of a series of hypotheses; there is, as it were, a sorites of abstract principles about ambition, and power, and reason, and affection; finally, a profound suspicion of Caesar is engendered, and his death is decreed. It is idealists who create a political terror; they are free from all desire for blood-shedding; but to them the lives of men and women are accidents; the lives of ideas are the true realities; and, armed with an abstract principle and a suspicion, they perform deeds which are at once beautiful and hideous:

> . . . 'tis a common proof,
> That lowliness is young ambition's ladder,
> Whereto the climber-upward turns his face;
> But when he once attains the utmost round,
> He then unto the ladder turns his back,
> Looks in the clouds, scorning the base degrees
> By which he did ascend: so Caesar may;
> Then, lest he may, prevent.

(II. 1. 21–8)

(Edward Dowden. *Shakspere: A Critical Study of His Mind and Art*, 1875)

The bloodbath

Killing people is a messy business and Shakespeare rarely leaves us in any doubt about that. 'Let us be sacrificers, but not butchers, Caius,' says Brutus, before the murder:

> We all stand up against the spirit of Caesar,
> And in the spirit of men there is no blood.
> O, that we then could come by Caesar's spirit,
> And not dismember Caesar! But, alas,
> Caesar must bleed for it.
>   (II. 1. 166–71)

And bleed he does, all over the stage, as the conspirators jostle one another for their turn at stabbing him. The text of the play doesn't indicate much about how the actual stabbing should be played, but that there was a great deal of blood about is made clear a little later in the scene, when Brutus actually invites his fellow conspirators to take part in a blood bath:

> Stoop, Romans, stoop,
> And let us bathe our hands in Caesar's blood
> Up to the elbows, and besmear our swords.
>   (III. 1. 105–7)

Alexander Pope, editing Shakespeare in the eighteenth century, was so sure that Shakespeare *couldn't* have meant Brutus to speak these lines, that he gave them to Casca. To justify this change he wrote: 'In all the editions, this speech is ascribed to Brutus, than which nothing is more inconsistent with his mild and philosophical character.' Most eighteenth- and nineteenth-century productions cut the incident and Brutus' lines out of the play altogether.

An American critic, Leo Kirschbaum, has pointed out that blood flowed freely on the Elizabethan stage:

The Elizabethans were familiar with scenes in which stage blood was liberally used. The tradition was old. In *Cambises* [1560s], 'Enter Cruelty and Murder with bloody hands.' They grasp their victim:

CRUELTY:
Even now I strike, his body to wound.
[Strike him in divers places.]
Beholde, now his blood springs out on the ground!
[A little bladder of vinegar prickt.]

Spectacular blood effects were created by painting, smearing, or sprinkling and by concealed bladders, sponges, and animal entrails. In *Locrine*, King Humber appears after the battle with 'his armes all bloodie'. In *Titus Andronicus*, Tamora's sons are bound. 'Enter Titus Andronicus with a knife, and Lavinia with a bason.' Then, 'He cuts their throats' on-stage . . . In Jonson's *Catiline*, the conspirators have their individual goblets filled from a bowl of mixed wine and blood. In *Appius and Virginia*, 'Enter Virginius with his knife, that and his arms stript up to the elbowes all bloudy.'

He remarks that Brutus' speech has often been taken to show that he is still trying to turn the murder of Caesar into a ritual, to persuade himself and the conspirators that they are 'sacrificers, but not butchers'. Does Brutus succeed in this attempt, as far as an audience is concerned? Kirschbaum doesn't think so:

That the dignified and gentle Brutus should propose the ghastly procedure of the conspirators bathing their hands in the blood of Caesar's body wrenches the mind. It emphasizes the disorder in the man. The major lesson of Shakespeare's history plays is so simple that its tremendous significance may be overlooked. It is this: *History is made by men.* How frightening this premise really becomes when we see the noble Brutus suddenly turn into a savage!
(L. Kirschbaum, 'Shakespeare's Stage Blood and its Critical Significance', *Proceedings of the Modern Language Association*, Vol. LXIV (1949) pp. 517–24)

Modern producers also have to decide how to play this central scene. Patrick Stewart, one of the contributors to the Capital Radio programme, describes here how it was handled in the production in which he played Cassius:

In any production of *Caesar*, there always comes a time when you have to sit down and face the problem of the assassination and what you do about the blood. I've seen productions where they avoided this altogether by not having blood at all, by imagining it. The principal reason is that if you're doing a play in repertory and you have a lot of blood flying about, unless you can afford to have new togas every night, you've got to provide spotlessly clean togas for curtain-up the next time you come to the performance. Well, we had three sets of togas each and so there was always one toga in the wardrobe, one toga on my back and one toga in the wash having the blood taken out of it. But much of the blood that will wash out doesn't look like blood, and the blood that does look like blood won't wash out. And we experimented with so many different formulas until finally, after we'd been running the play for some time, they came up with something that was absolutely spot-on. And we used it for weeks, and it worked splendidly – it looked real, it actually congealed like real blood, and it washed out. And then one matinee we came to the assassination and Casca said, 'Speak hands for me!' and stabbed at Caesar's neck. All the conspirators were provided with kind of washing-up liquid bottles – some very tiny ones, some quite large ones, you know, the economy size – somewhere tucked away inside their toga. And, surrounding Caesar, one by one we would stab and hack and attack him, squeezing at the same time, so the blood really flew. It spurted across the stage. In fact we used to get cleaning bills from the audience because the blood used to go out into them. But on this particular afternoon, Casca stabbed and squeezed and, as he squeezed, a stench began to fill the stage and, as we all began to squeeze, the stench got worse and worse and worse, so that I was on the point of vomiting. We had to play through all of the scene with this appalling smell everywhere. It was the kind of thing you get when a kid lets off a stink bomb somewhere. We couldn't understand it. We got off and complained about this smell, where was it coming from, and then they told us the story. The blood we had been using for all those weeks was real blood. It was from the abattoir and it had been frozen. And for some reason, either the freezer had broken down or there had been some problem, and the blood we had used that afternoon had gone off, was bad. We didn't use real blood again after that.

A Midsummer Night's Dream

MICHAEL ASPEL:

You probably realize that a silly story can contain much serious suggestion; even the funniest, zaniest book can help you face certain situations, can help you make real decisions about, for example, your relationship with your parents. Perhaps it is a bit easier to learn when the last page leaves you laughing rather than with a lump in your throat; in a good mood we can all take a little self-criticism – the euphoria may not last very long but it's useful while it's there. Now talking of seeing yourself in a story, you might see some unflattering reflections in *A Midsummer Night's Dream*. The chances are, though, that the magic of this comedy will put you under its spell. Diana Rigg recalls the first time she acted Shakespeare's tale of the problematic path of love and marriage; she was twenty; the production was in Stratford.

DIANA RIGG:

The joke about Stratford is that most men, when they go to Stratford, carry a spear. I think I can claim to be the only *woman* who went to Stratford and carried a spear, and that was in *A Midsummer Night's Dream*. I was cast as one of Hippolyta's attendants and it was the designer's bright idea (although I considered it thoroughly ignominious) to make us as butch as possible, so there I was with a helmet and armour on and carrying a spear. It gave me a wonderful opportunity then to listen to the lines (because that's the only thing that you can do if you're standing around on a stage) and I grew to love them. I was absolutely fascinated too by the audience's reaction. They were as enchanted as the play – it deals with fairies and that is synonymous with enchantment.

MICHAEL ASPEL:

Yes, this is the play where Oberon and Titania, king and queen of the fairies, flit through the dark wood beyond Athens – the same wood in which Bottom and his workmates meet to rehearse a play – and this is where four young lovers grow to a greater maturity and understanding of love after a mad night, or perhaps a nightmare, in the wood. When the play starts, Duke Theseus of Athens is planning his wedding party with his bride-to-be, Hippolyta. So one wedding is in the offing. We soon hear plans of another, when Egeus, a nobleman, interrupts the Duke. Egeus comes to complain about his daughter, Hermia. Hermia loves Lysander and refuses to marry his rival, Demetrius, her father's choice for her. The Duke recommends Hermia to obey her father; Hermia and Lysander feel they have no choice but to elope that very night. They confide their plan to Helena. Helena is painfully and unrequitedly in love with Demetrius. It's one of those 'she loves him but he doesn't love her' situations. Germaine Greer wrote her doctoral thesis on Shakespeare's early comedies.

GERMAINE GREER:

Hermia says that if she can't marry Lysander (she can't give any good reason why she should, except that she's in love with him), then she'll become a nun. Chastity (Diana) and sexual love (Cupid) are seen to be in opposition, and at the beginning of the play we have a destructive situation.

MICHAEL ASPEL:

One element of the play that interests Terry Neil is how the characters are forced into adopting roles. Once one character behaves unnaturally, a whole chain of role-playing begins.

TERRY NEIL:

By this I mean, not just people being actors on the stage, but the actors themselves performing certain definite roles. Think of Egeus, for example, acting out the heavy father to begin with, and insisting that his choice shall be the one that his daughter accepts and how, as a consequence of this, Theseus has to perform his duty as a law-upholder in Athens. This, in turn, forces the lovers to flee, and Helena, acting against type and hoping to win favour with Demetrius, to play the role of the informer.

DIANA RIGG:

The second time I was in *A Midsummer Night's Dream*, I played Helena and I identified very much with her. First of all because I was a tall adolescent – I was clumsy and I was ugly – and nobody, no boy, liked me particularly. This is poor Helena's case. She is mad about Demetrius, and Demetrius only cares for lovely, pretty, small, tidy, thoroughly complacent, Hermia. And I felt that very strongly – as an adolescent, I was an outcast as well – so it had enormous meaning for me. I think adolescence is a period of pain. Those of you in adolescence, the unlucky ones, perhaps you will be able to identify with what I'm talking about.

MICHAEL ASPEL:

Perhaps you can. In real life that story of misery does often sort itself out in time but Shakespeare can't afford to wait because he only has our attention for the few hours that we, as an audience, have to spare. So he needs a catalyst, something that'll make the young lovers grow up rather more quickly than is usual. That's what happens when the lovers go to the wood. It's a trick he uses in other comedies – you'll recognize it if you know *As You Like It*. People go into Shakespeare's forests a bit confused and disorganized, but when they come out they're mature. Our young lovers aren't the only characters to go to the wood. The rude mechanics – Bottom, and Snug, and Peter Quince, and Snout – arrange to rehearse a play in the wood. They hope to perform it at the Duke's wedding. They're clowns really, but they do fit neatly into this play about love because they're rehearsing the tragic love story of Pyramus and Thisbe. But Bottom and his mates are mainly there to make us laugh, and Shakespeare introduces them just before we can get too serious about the lovers.

TIMOTHY WEST:

It's a very diverse play. It seems at first to be constructed of three different unrelated elements that come together, perhaps rather crudely, at the end. You've got the clowns – I think you should found them on the worst amateur dramatic society you've ever seen because that's who they were meant to be, and there's not a lot of exaggeration in some of them: the man who wants to play everything; the producer who feels his grip slipping away from him; the man who cannot possibly learn lines; the other man who is too old to play anything but has to be there, because he always has been. They're wonderful characters, and the interplay between them is marvellous in the rehearsal scenes.

PUPIL:

When I saw the play, I thought Bottom was a good sort of bloke; he was like the people of today – an ordinary man.

MICHAEL ASPEL:

Yes, you wouldn't be surprised to meet Bottom today flogging his gear down Petticoat Lane. And it's not surprising to hear this comment on the next characters to hold the stage.

PUPIL:

A Midsummer Night's Dream is a play full of fairies – it's got nothing to do with the twentieth century.

EILEEN ATKINS:

I don't think that. I don't know about you, but I tend to think if it's a dreadful day, that the stars must be in the wrong conjunction, or something like that. So I don't think it's too odd to think that if the king and the queen of the fairies are quarrelling, then everything goes wrong. Titania is the fairy queen – but the squabbles she has with Oberon are really showing you human squabbles.

MICHAEL ASPEL:

Squabbles of some kind are certainly what Oberon and Titania are having. They argue over a small boy who is the son of a dear, but dead, friend of Titania. Their whole marriage has come adrift and their estrangement brings terrible storms into the human world. These fairies are intimately connected with our world – they aren't pretty little tinkerbells. If today it's hard for us to take them seriously, try being the actor. Here's Patrick Stewart, who has played Oberon, the king of the fairies.

PATRICK STEWART:

There are problems attached to playing a fairy that don't exist in any other part; for one thing you have to convince an audience that you are something other than mortal and, from the beginning of this production, we concentrated on those aspects of the character that were super-normal. Because we live in an age when the fairies at the bottom of your garden are not as real for us as they might have been maybe only a hundred years ago, we had to find something which would have some kind of significance for an audience in the 1970s. Looking at Oberon's actions in the play, he is a creature who can exist both in the human and in the fairy world. This potential that he has, for being both insubstantial fairy and human being, is at the root of the conflict between Titania and himself. Titania herself has become too closely involved with the human world, and Oberon is jealous of that.

EILEEN ATKINS:

'Why should Titania cross her Oberon?/I do but beg a little changeling boy/To be my henchman.' That is, he's saying – All I want is the boy. And she says, 'Set your heart at rest./The fairy land buys not the child of me./His mother was a votaress of my order,/. . ./And for her sake do I rear up her boy;/And for her sake I will not part with him.'

MICHAEL ASPEL:

So Titania refuses her husband's request, which was a selfish one anyway, and he decides to take his revenge. He orders Puck, his servant, to gather a plant which has magic powers. If the juice is squeezed into the eyes of someone who is asleep, it will cause him or her to fall in love with the first creature he sees when he wakes up. Oberon puts some into Titania's eyes and, to be quite sure of his evil plan working, he chants, 'Wake when some vile thing is near.' Meanwhile Oberon has seen Helena and Demetrius quarrelling. Eileen Atkins recalls the first time she came across this quarrelsome couple; she was introduced to them by her elocution master.

EILEEN ATKINS:

All he said to me was; 'Now this girl's in love with this man, and he doesn't fancy her at all, and you're absolutely mad about him and he doesn't like you, and he's just said these awful, rude things to you and left you.' I just read it – I didn't even know it was verse – and I said, 'This is marvellous, it's exactly how you feel.' And because he didn't tell me then 'Shakespeare!' – this was just a girl whose man didn't fancy her.

MICHAEL ASPEL:

He will soon. Oberon orders Puck to spray a little juice into the young Athenian's eyes. How was Puck to know that the young, Athenian man sleeping none too near an Athenian maid was Lysander, respecting the chastity of his Hermia? Who should wake Lysander but Helena, with whom he promptly falls in love? Confusion reigns. Well, now let's pick Terry Neil's brain again. Perhaps there's another element to hold on to.

TERRY NEIL:

Think of harmony and discord in the play. And notice, too, how they tend to set up chain reactions – one bit of discord leads to another. Egeus opposes Lysander, so he flees with Hermia; the lovers confront each other and wrangle in the woods as a consequence. The attempts by Oberon, who is himself by no means in a contented state of mind, to resolve the situation, fail at first.

GERMAINE GREER:

Oberon is our own power to fantasize and delude ourselves. You must see that that can be terribly dangerous.

MICHAEL ASPEL:

And so is the wood where Hermia awakes to find herself alone. Now don't imagine that because there are fairies in this wood it's a pretty place for a picnic. As I said, there are no tinkerbells. You're expected to find it scarey. Here's another favourite question: 'What does the wood gain or lose when it's made to seem dark and sinister?'

GERMAINE GREER:

You must get the feeling, I think, that the wood is the inside of somebody's head, and they're chasing round and round. Sometimes it seems to be dazzling and misty, and other times it seems to be dark and terrifying. So you could wake up crying out that you thought a serpent was at your bosom (which is of course a sexual image).

Shakespeare, in this play, shows you love as a sort of delusion, a sort of accident, and puts it down to the influence of Oberon and Cupid's flower which has its own story, of destructive sexual passion. This flower, when put on the eyes of Titania, makes her fall in love with the first thing she sees, which is an ass. An ass is a very good way of referring to plain beastly sexual appetite. The ass is supposed to have the largest sexual organ in relation to its overall size of any common animal. So Titania, the bodyless and beautiful, is hopelessly besotted by something gross and base, like some young woman who has simply fallen in love with the first man she ever met, because all that's operating in her is neat sexuality.

MICHAEL ASPEL:

Which so delights Oberon, her husband, that once again he decides to interfere with the mortals. Remember Lysander is now in love with Helena, who is in love with Demetrius, who is in love with Hermia, who is not in love with him. Oberon squeezes some of his magic plant into Demetrius' eyes.

DIANA RIGG:

Then the miracle happens. Demetrius and Lysander turn round and adore Helena. For the first time in her life, she finds herself an object of admiration. She's no fool – she obviously thinks it's a terrible game, and fun at her expense, because she knows the truth of the situation. And there ensues a wonderful battle between Helena and Hermia, when Hermia learns what it's like to be not loved. The two of them have a right old set-to.

MICHAEL ASPEL:

Most of the folly happens during the night, which is a good time for dreams.

PATRICK STEWART:

Puck, towards the end of the night, sees the first light of dawn in the sky – because he is a creature of the night it alarms him, and he tells Oberon that the time has come for them to wind up this whole night's fantasy and to flee the day. And he's afraid of what might happen if they don't. Oberon comforts him and reassures him, and he says:

> OBERON
> But we are spirits of another sort.
> I with the morning's love have oft made sport,
> And like a forester the groves may tread
> Even till the eastern gate all fiery red
> Opening on Neptune with fair blessèd beams
> Turns into yellow gold his salt green streams.
>   (III. 2. 388–93)

A few minutes later, another human comes on to the stage – the other authority figure in the play, Theseus. And his first line, to one of the huntsmen, is 'Go, one of you; find out the forester.' Why did Shakespeare choose that kind of person for Theseus to ask for? There's so much that he could have selected and he chooses 'forester' where a scene and a half earlier Oberon has himself described himself as being a forester in the wood. And one gets a shimmering sense of these two figures, Theseus and Oberon, having contact in the forest – that there has been a time when Oberon, as a forester, has met and associated with Theseus.

TERRY NEIL:

And then when Theseus hears that the lovers are reconciled and all are happy, he promptly overrules Egeus and the happy group gather.

DIANA RIGG:

They get together. But in the getting together, they learn something terribly important. When they come out of the forest, they're adults. They've left behind them the excesses of love and jealousy and they have a kind of objectivity about them which means that they are infinitely more mature. I think you can find the summation of this in the speeches that happen when Theseus and Hippolyta and Egeus leave and the four lovers are left together on the stage. Demetrius says, 'These things seem small and undistinguishable,/Like far-off mountains turned into clouds,' and Hermia says, 'Methinks I see these things with parted eye;/When everything seems double.' And Helena says, 'So methinks,/And I have found Demetrius, like a jewel,/Mine own and not mine own.' When she says 'mine own and not mine own', she realizes for the first time that when you love somebody, it doesn't mean to say that they are yours. It means that you can take steps back, and look at them, and evaluate them, and love them for what they are, but not necessarily for being joined to you.

TIMOTHY WEST:

A Midsummer Night's Dream has also of course got its elements of cruelty in it, and the scene where the layabouts in the court at the end totally muck up the performance of *Pyramus and Thisbe* is an appalling thing. Though people say, 'Well, of course, it must have been quite like that in the Elizabethan theatre', it's equally true to say that the actors, and indeed Shakespeare, can't have enjoyed it much. I think it's very clear whose side Shakespeare's on.

MICHAEL ASPEL:

We can enjoy those characters despite the attempted sabotage of their play, *Pyramus and Thisbe*, by the three newly-wed couples – that's Theseus and Hippolyta, Lysander and Hermia, Demetrius and Helena. They can hardly wait for bedtime to solemnize their love, which makes a healthy contrast with the heroic, but sterile, love of Pyramus and Thisbe, divided first by a wall and finally by death.

GERMAINE GREER:

It is the old idea, I suppose, of heroic love which ends in death. Shakespeare's more interested in heroic love which ends in life which founds a family and which goes onward. You might pay particular attention to the fairy song at the end of the play – it's actually about having children which is, of course, the great marriage blessing. Now, it's not often realized that, for Shakespeare, marriage was not a cliché ending to a story. Because we now think that all stories end with marriage and happily-ever-after, it comes as a bit of a surprise to realize that, before Shakespeare's time marriage was not a theme in literature. People did not write stories about marriage; they wrote stories about adultery, and stories about love and war, but they didn't write stories about the biggest story, for us, of how people set up house together and make it work.

DIANA RIGG:

I think he was being much more subtle than just writing a play about marriage. He was writing a play about love and about the course of love that leads up to marriage and what can happen within marriage as well – the battle between Oberon and Titania.

GERMAINE GREER:

The struggle between chastity and sexuality, between Diana and Cupid, has to be resolved in this case by a kind of ritual solution in which one character, Demetrius, is still the victim of Cupid's flower, because he was in love with the wrong person. He has got to be turned round and made to love somebody who loves him. That's done, in this case, by witchcraft. And the witchcraft stays there – he is married bewitched. Now that ought to frighten you.

PATRICK STEWART:

I think *A Midsummer Night's Dream* is a most serious play and has been perhaps unfairly considered as a bit of light entertainment. Those dark areas of anger and jealousy, of lust and hatred, infect all the characters in the play, none of them are spared it. Everybody in the play, every single character, every major character, learns some kind of lesson in *A Midsummer Night's Dream*. They all go through an experience which changes them.

DIANA RIGG:

Hermia learnt a lesson by not being wanted. She learnt how it felt to be an outcast. The boys who were rivals learnt friendship afterwards. And Helena learnt what it was like to be the belle of the ball for once in her life. That did her an enormous amount of good because she became altogether calmer afterwards, instead of behaving with the frenetic activity of somebody who's utterly rejected.

MICHAEL ASPEL:

You could take this play as nothing more than a pretty tribute, written to celebrate the wedding of an aristocratic pair of Elizabethans, and of course if you can back this up with evidence from the text, your opinion is as good as anyone else's. But you must agree that it is interesting to look for reflections of our own lives in stories written long ago. I think the title of this play is suggestive of something more subtle. It isn't just any dream, but a midsummer night dream. Midsummer is traditionally the time when we all go a little bit mad. Remember love is 'said to be a child/Because in choice he is so oft beguiled'.

TERRY NEIL:

Love may be a child, may even force characters sometimes to behave in ridiculous ways, but nonetheless it remains the goal that all aim at. If the play of *A Midsummer Night's Dream* has any kind of moral in it this is it, and it's certainly not a heavy moral.

EILEEN ATKINS:

I think it's a most beautiful play, absolutely beautiful, and everybody should have a smile on their face or there's something wrong with the production.

A play for a wedding

Critics and historians seem fairly sure that *A Midsummer Night's Dream* was written for an actual occasion, the wedding of an important lord and lady. It has never been definitely discovered whose wedding Shakespeare was writing the play for, but there are two or three clear possibilities. It was normal for a marriage feast for the wealthy to end with an entertainment of some kind; just as Theseus and Hippolyta's wedding celebrations end with the play of Pyramus and Thisbe. It adds flavour to the last act of the play if you imagine the just-married aristocratic couple on stage being watched by the just-married aristocratic couple in the audience.

When Theseus is choosing the entertainment for his wedding party he asks the master of ceremonies:

> . . . what abridgement have you for this evening?
> What masque, what music?
>
> (V. 1. 39–40)

Masques were special kinds of plays which were designed to entertain private audiences on important occasions like court weddings. A masque usually had rather a thin plot, and involved a good deal of singing, dancing and spectacle. It often contained references to the particular occasion on which it was being performed, and compliments to the important people present. Masques began by being little more than processions of dancers ('masquers'), who acted out short dramatic interludes as they processed round a hall, but they gradually became much more elaborate and lengthy. The costumes became more fantastic, the staging more ambitious, and the scenic effects more technically complicated and impressive to watch. In the early seventeenth century there was a performance of a masque in which Hell's mouth, flaming and smoking 'unto the top of the roof' was shown on the stage, and of another in which a huge sea-shell, carrying the Queen and her ladies, and drawn by sea-monsters, sailed across the stage on imitation waves.

A Midsummer Night's Dream is a play rather than a masque. It does not rely on fantastic costumes, music, lighting or special effects for its power. Indeed, Peter Brook's RSC production in 1970 proved that it could be played on a stage that was virtually bare. But through poetry Shakespeare does create a world of music and fairyland which is just as magical as any more elaborately staged spectacle.

In one aspect the play is reminiscent of a masque: in its emphasis on dancing. The fairies perform two dances in the course of the play, and Quince and his company end their performance with a 'Bergomask dance'. The plot, too, has something dance-like about it. During the night in the wood the lovers' comings and goings are as highly patterned as a folk dance in which the dancers combine and re-combine – and everyone joins up with the right partner at the end.

> Up and down, up and down,
> I will lead them up and down
> (III. 2. 396–7)

sings Puck, and this is what Shakespeare does as he leads his characters through the complicated pattern of his plot.

'The most lamentable comedy, and most cruel death of Pyramus and Thisbe'

In two or three of his plays, Shakespeare presents a 'play within the play'. He nearly always reveals something of his own ideas about the theatre when he does so. The 'mechanicals' play' in _Midsummer Night's Dream_ is a parody of a kind of tragedy that Shakespeare's audience would have found a bit old-fashioned; but it is more than just a theatrical skit.

The lovers who sit round laughing in such a sophisticated way at the passionate love speeches of Pyramus and Thisbe were proclaiming their own ardent feelings just as wildly in the wood not long before. Though the events of *Pyramus and Thisbe* are not the same as those of *A Midsummer Night's Dream* (they are closer to *Romeo and Juliet*), there are things that the play and the play-within-the-play have in common. The parents of Pyramus and Thisbe oppose their love, just as Egeus had opposed Hermia's love for Lysander. The lovers flee into the forest for a secret assignation; so had Hermia and Lysander. Pyramus and Thisbe's 'cruel death' is different from the Athenian lovers' fate, but all of them have been part of 'lamentable comedies'. Just as the audience laughed at the confusion and anger and misery of the Athenian lovers in the wood, so now the lovers sit, amused and detached, passing remarks about the play.

Pyramus and Thisbe would have reminded Shakespeare's audience of old melodramas they had seen. The style is ridiculously exaggerated, the verse thumps along, and dramatic conventions are heavily parodied – like Pyramus explaining at length that he is dying:

> Now am I dead,
> Now am I fled;
> My soul is in the sky.
> Tongue, lose thy light;
> Moon, take thy flight;
> Now die, die, die, die, die.
> (V. 1. 293–8)

The style of acting varies from the simply incompetent – Peter Quince understands so little of his Prologue that he makes nonsense of it by getting all the full stops in the wrong places – to the overacting of Bottom. The part of Pyramus pretty well demands a ranting, old-fashioned style of delivery:

> O grim-looked night, O night with hue so black,
> O night which ever art when day is not!
> O night, O night, alack, alack, alack,
> I fear my Thisbe's promise is forgot.
> (V. 1. 167–70)

Less self-confident actors, like Moonshine, are completely thrown by the endless interruptions from their fashionable audience.

The staging of the play, which causes the actors to rack their brains so much, is another in-joke. Quince and his company debate the difficulties of bringing a wall and moonlight on to the stage, and finally get round the problem in an absurd fashion, by casting actors to play Wall and Moonshine. Shakespeare, meantime, has been effortlessly representing woods and fairies, moonlight and sunrise, with nothing to help him but words.

While they try to make some things more real, Quince and his company are anxious to make other things *less* real. The lion that is supposed to frighten Thisbe causes them much concern – will it also frighten the audience? They solve this problem by inserting in the play yet another laborious speech of explanation, to be spoken by the actor playing the lion.

> You ladies – you whose gentle hearts do fear
>   The smallest monstrous mouse that creeps on floor –
> May now, perchance, both quake and tremble here,
>   When Lion rough in wildest rage doth roar.
> Then know that I as Snug the joiner am
> A lion fell, nor else no lion's dam,
> For if I should as lion come in strife
> Into this place, 'twere pity on my life.
>
> (V. 1. 215–22)

This may be a topical joke. In August 1594, a pageant at the Scottish court was to have included a lion drawing a triumphal chariot. But because of fears that the lion would alarm the ladies present, this part of the pageant was left out.

The audience for the play is hard to please and extremely bad-mannered too. They keep up a constant stream of heckling, which sometimes brings the performance to a standstill. In Shakespeare's theatre it was smart to buy a seat on the stage itself if one was a rich theatre-goer. The following mock advice from an Elizabethan writer probably gives some idea of how fashionable members of Shakespeare's audience behaved:

It shall crown you with rich commendation to laugh aloud in the middest of the most serious and saddest scene of the terriblest tragedy: and to let that clapper [your tongue] be tost so high that all the house may ring of it.

So there they must have sat, cracking jokes and nuts, very like Shakespeare's Athenians.

Only Theseus is gracious and charitable enough to take the performance in the spirit in which it is meant and to point out the similarity between Quince's company's efforts and the highest dramatic art. All are pale imitations of real life:

The best in this kind are but shadows; and the worst are no worse, if imagination amend them.

(V. 1. 208–9)

The wording of Puck's epilogue ('If we shadows have offended . . .') recall Theseus' speech, and remind us of what Shakespeare's company and Quince's company have in common.

Midsummer madness

Thou toldest me they were stolen unto this wood,
And here am I, and wood within this wood
Because I cannot meet my Hermia.

(II. 1. 191–3)

'Wood' was an old word for 'mad'. When Demetrius tells Helena, in the wood outside Athens, that he is mad, mad with love, he speaks for several of the characters. The wood is a timeless kind of place where anything can happen, like the woods in fairy stories. It's also dangerous. Demetrius threatens the persistent Helena, 'I shall do thee mischief in the wood'; there are wild beasts in the darkness. But the main danger is that of being maddened or misled, as Lysander and Demetrius are, or transformed physically, like Bottom.

. . . to say the truth, reason and love keep little company together nowadays.

(III. 1. 136–7)

It is Oberon and his agent Puck who engineer all this confusion. The name of the little flower, which they use as a love-potion, 'love-in-idleness', would have meant 'love-madness' to the Elizabethans. Love has often been described as a sort of insanity, and slang uses that idea colloquially a lot; people say 'she's mad about him', and sing 'I'm crazy about my baby, and my baby's crazy 'bout me'. The sort of love that comes out of the blue, that transforms the personality, that is an antisocial sort of monomania, is the sort of love that infects Demetrius, Lysander and Titania in the course of the night in the wood. In Titania's case the love object is ugly and ridiculous, and her love is seen to be a complete delusion. It has all been real midsummer madness.

> Things base and vile, holding no quantity,
> Love can transpose to form and dignity.
> Love looks not with the eyes, but with the mind,
> And therefore is winged Cupid painted blind.
> Nor hath love's mind of any judgement taste;
> Wings and no eyes figure unheedy haste.
> And therefore is love said to be a child
> Because in choice he is so oft beguiled.
>
> (I. 1. 232–9)

Lost in the wood

A Midsummer Night's Dream is a kind of fairytale. In this passage, Bruno Bettelheim describes what woods often mean in fairytales:

In many European fairy tales the brother who leaves soon finds himself in a deep, dark forest, where he feels lost, having given up the organization of his life which the parental home provided, and not yet having built up the inner structures which we develop only under the impact of life experiences we have to master more or less on our own. Since ancient times the near-impenetrable forest in which we get lost has symbolized the dark, hidden, near-impenetrable world of our unconscious. If we have lost the framework which gave structure to our past life and must now find our own way to become ourselves, and have entered this wilderness with an as yet undeveloped personality,

when we succeed in finding our way out we shall emerge with a much more highly developed humanity.
(Bruno Bettelheim, *The Uses of Enchantment*, Thames & Hudson, 1976)

A fairy tale

Shakespeare's fairies are not pretty little gossamer creatures with wings, they are mischievous and sometimes frightening spirits, which Shakespeare would have known about through the many folk tales and superstitions that were common knowledge both in Warwickshire, where he came from, and in other parts of England. Puck, or Robin Goodfellow, was thought of as a particularly malicious kind of sprite, like the Brownie in this old fairy story:

THE CAULD LAD OF HILTON

At Hilton Hall, long years ago, there lived a Brownie that was the contrariest Brownie you ever knew. At night, after the servants had gone to bed, it would turn everything topsy-turvy, put sugar in the salt cellars, pepper into the beer, and was up to all kinds of pranks. It would throw the chairs down, put tables on their backs, rake out fires, and do as much mischief as could be. But sometimes it would be in a good temper, and then! – 'What's a Brownie?' you say. Oh, it's a kind of a sort of a Bogle, but it isn't so cruel as a Redcap! What! you don't know what's a Bogle or a Redcap! Ah me! what's the world a-coming to? Of course, a Brownie is a funny little thing, half man, half goblin, with pointed ears and hairy hide. When you bury a treasure, you scatter over it blood drops of a newly slain kid or lamb, or, better still, bury the animal with the treasure, and a Brownie will watch over it for you, and frighten everybody else away.

Where was I? Well, as I was a-saying, the Brownie at Hilton Hall would play at mischief, but if the servants laid out for it a bowl of cream, or a knucklecake spread with honey, it would clear away things for them, and make everything tidy in the kitchen. One night, however, when the servants had stopped up late, they heard a noise in the kitchen, and, peeping in, saw the Brownie swinging to and fro on the Jack chain, and saying:

> 'Woe's me! woe's me!
> The acorn's not yet
> Fallen from the tree,
> That's to grow the wood,
> That's to make the cradle,
> That's to rock the bairn,
> That's to grow to the man,
> That's to lay me.
> Woe's me! Woe's me!'

So they took pity on the poor Brownie, and asked the nearest hen-wife what they should do to send it away. 'That's easy enough,' said the hen-wife, and told them that a Brownie that's paid for its service, in aught that's not perishable, goes away at once. So they made a cloak of Lincoln green, with a hood to it, and put it by the hearth and watched. They saw the Brownie come up, and seeing the hood and cloak, put them on and frisk about, dancing on one leg and saying:

> 'I've taken your cloak, I've taken your hood;
> The Cauld Lad of Hilton will do no more good.'

And with that it vanished, and was never seen or heard of afterwards.

Suggestions for staging

If *A Midsummer Night's Dream* was first performed at a court wedding celebration, it was probably staged in a big private house. Sir Arthur Quiller-Couch's suggestions for staging the play may help us to visualize the first performance:

... I once discussed with a friend how, if given our will, we would have *A Midsummer Night's Dream* presented. We agreed at length on this:

The set scene should represent a large Elizabethan hall, panelled, having a lofty oak-timbered roof and an enormous staircase. The cavity under the staircase, occupying in breadth two-thirds of the stage, should be fronted with folding or sliding doors, which, being opened, should reveal the wood, recessed, moonlit, with its trees upon a flat arras or tapestry. On this secondary remoter stage the lovers should wander through their adventures, the fairies now conspiring in the quiet hall under the lantern, anon withdrawing into the woodland to befool the mortals straying there. Then, for the last scene and the interlude of *Pyramus and Thisbe*, the hall should be filled with lights and company. That over, the bridal couples go up the great staircase. Last of all – and after a long pause, when the house is quiet, the lantern all but extinguished, the hall looking vast and eerie, lit only by a last flicker from the hearth – the fairies, announced by Puck, should come tripping back, swarming forth from cupboards and down curtains, somersaulting downstairs, sliding down the baluster rails; all hushed as they fall to work with their brooms – hushed, save for one little voice and a thin, small chorus scarcely more audible than the last dropping embers:

> Through the house give glimmering light
>   By the dead and drowsy fire;
> Every elf and fairy sprite
>   Hop as light as bird from briar . . .
> Hand in hand with fairy grace
> Will we sing and bless this place.
>   Trip away,
>   Make no stay,
> Meet me all by break of day.

(*Shakespeare's Workmanship*, Cambridge University Press, 1923.)

Brook's '*Dream*'

The most famous production of *A Midsummer Night's Dream* in recent years was directed by Peter Brook for the Royal Shakespeare Company. The newspaper review that follows gives some idea of the impact of that production:

BROOK BREAK-THROUGH IN '*Dream*'
John Barber

In a production of *A Midsummer Night's Dream* that will surely make theatre history, Peter Brook last night at Stratford-on-Avon tore through all conventional ideas about how the play should be staged.

He found new ways of giving form to its latent poetry and power.

For setting he offers a dazzling white box. The actors too, wear white – or else plain colours as vivid as a conjuror's silks. The only furniture is four cushions, also white.

Several trapezes hang from the flies. Iron ladders at each side of the stage extend to a railed platform where musicians, zither, guitar or bongo-drums are stationed.

The naked harshness of this environment is used by Mr Brook as a means of exposing the actor's words and emotions. Its coldness suits the palace scenes admirably, and we are at once seized by the pathetic vehemence of the lovers' protests.

And when the rude mechanicals come on, the white courtyard is exactly right for a gang – it might be their lunch-hour – in flat caps, string vests and braces. Here suddenly Bottom, refused the role of the Lion, downs tools and sulkily walks off the stage and up the theatre aisle.

It is one of many stunning effects. The midnight wood is created with a galaxy of tricks. The trees are steel spirals held on fishing rods from above, and in the helical coils the lovers will be enmeshed.

Above, the fairies scrape washerboards and shake thunder-sheets to give the wood its awesome sounds. Oberon's enchanted herb is represented by a silver dish spinning on a wand, and passed from Oberon's wand to Puck's when both are on trapezes.

And when Titania sees Bottom translated, suddenly Mendelssohn's Wedding March blares forth and the stage fills with confetti the size of plates. In any description, such devices must sound mere gimmickry. I can only report that they held me enthralled as the mood of the play leapt – one never knew what would happen next – from horseplay to startling bawdry, from poetic dignity to seething eroticism and to alarming chases up and down the ladders.

Old lines whose familiarity had bored one for years came up fresh and comic or distressingly apt.

For it was Mr Brook's triumph to generate an atmosphere in which only the poetry mattered. Alan Howard, doubling Theseus and Oberon, discovered a new high dignity. The lovers, who seemed without wigs or even make-up and who often broke into song when the lines rhymed, were as exposed and as distraught as modern adolescents.

(*Daily Telegraph*, 1970)

Twelfth Night

(in order of appearance)

Michael Aspel	*presenter*
Judi Dench	*actress*
Eileen Atkins	*actress*
Timothy West	*actor*
Donald Sinden	*actor*
Janet Suzman	*actress*
John Barton	*director*
John Cleese	*writer/actor*
Tony O'Sullivan	*teacher*

MICHAEL ASPEL:

Humour can take many different forms. It can be savage or silly, uproarious or just an undertone. Laughter and learning are the love and marriage of literature. They go hand in hand in *Twelfth Night*.

JUDI DENCH:

I did a production of *Twelfth Night* at Stratford, with John Barton. There was a marvellous picture of Orsino at the very beginning of the play. It starts, 'If music be the food of love, play on.' I've always thought it must be difficult for an actor to walk on to a stage and say, 'If music be the food of love, play on,' when probably the person who is playing has been only playing for a couple of minutes. So the play used to go on at 7.30 – and we used to have Orsino sitting on the stage when the audience were coming in, in a darkened chamber with a lot of candles guttering; you could hear the musician playing and singing. This young prince, who was obviously so in love that he didn't bother with his clothes very much, was sitting in a chair in a marvellous long dressing gown which looked a bit tatty, because he obviously hadn't changed it for a long time. He'd grown a lovelock and was very unshaven. When the audience came in they were always rather hushed because you had this wonderful music going on, and obviously somebody was in a kind of reverie. He hid his face – he didn't sit in a romantic way, he sat rather hunched up. And then, when at last the lights in the audience faded, the lights on the stage came up very slightly and in the guttering candlelight you heard the young man saying to the musician, who had stopped playing, 'If music be the food of love, play on,/Give me excess of it.' Somehow it made enormous sense – it was wonderful.

MICHAEL ASPEL:

The Duke Orsino is a young nobleman with nothing to do all day but lie around sighing about his unrequited love for Olivia. Her day is even less fun. She's decided to go into seven years' mourning for her recently dead brother. Now, if Orsino and Olivia were the only characters in *Twelfth Night*, they'd probably be living alone and unloved to this day. But it's no longer any secret that, by the end of *Twelfth Night*, they are each happily married. This is because one day a young lady called Viola is shipwrecked on the island where they live. Here's Judi Dench again.

JUDI DENCH:

Viola, which is the part I played, is a kind of catalyst in the play. She's the one who gets everything moving. It's a play about everybody being in love with each other.

MICHAEL ASPEL:

Yes, there's a lot of love about. So much, in fact, that in the past examiners have wanted to know about it. They've asked, for example, this question: '"What is love? 'Tis not hereafter;/Present mirth hath present laughter" – Is this a description of love in the play?' So look out for suggestions on this. Is the love courtly or comic, honest or hopeless? Is it sisterly or self-love? You'll find it all on the island of Illyria.

JUDI DENCH:

And on to this island is swept Viola. She suddenly thinks that she's a woman and she's on her own, and it's not very safe for a girl to be wandering about on her own. So she decides to dress up as a boy and see if she can get a job, with Orsino. Then in the next scene, lo and behold, she's fallen in love with Orsino.

MICHAEL ASPEL:

Viola changes her name to Cesario. With her dressed as a boy, and in love with a boy, things are going to get complicated. It's lucky that we have three Violas to help out – Judi Dench, Eileen Atkins and Janet Suzman. The sad thing about Viola is that she is the character who knows what love is. She knows you have to grab love when you can because 'youth's a stuff will not endure'. But how can she, dressed as a boy? And even Viola isn't foolproof, far from it. The man she loves is a bit feeble. Eileen Atkins feels strongly for Viola at this point.

EILEEN ATKINS:

Why has my best friend fallen in love with that idiot? He's so conceited, he's such a fool and he's in love with that other absolute idiot. That is life, isn't it? The most beautiful, perfect girl doesn't fall for the most beautiful, perfect, nice, sensible man; she usually falls for some idiot who thinks he's frightfully good-looking, and that's about it.

MICHAEL ASPEL:

Well, there's a familiar syndrome. Viola isn't ridiculous, she's just very real. Before you write her off as a daft female, remember that the examiners ask this sort of question about her: 'Viola is the only person who can be taken seriously. Discuss.' At which point you need to ask yourself how seriously you should take a crowd of characters who appear and reappear throughout the play. These are the relatives and servants of Olivia: her drunken uncle, Sir Toby; his bumbling friend, Sir Andrew Aguecheek, who wants to marry Olivia; Maria, Olivia's lively but spiteful maid, who wants to marry Sir Toby; Feste, Olivia's clown, who sings some melodic and melancholy songs; and, of course, there's Malvolio, Olivia's pompous, priggish yet proficient steward.

TIMOTHY WEST:

Twelfth Night is, I think, one of the great comedies of all time. The reason I say that is because all the characters are very serious people, which is the essence of comedy. Sir Toby and Sir Andrew, who are responsible for the broad comedy of the play, and Feste – all people who are living under a great threat, I mean, the threat of the withdrawal of patronage. Because of this I think there's a temptation to make the play a very autumnal, Chekhovian kind of comedy with the odd, polite giggle. But this is totally wrong. Obviously Shakespeare wanted these people to be very funny, and he wanted Malvolio, which is the only character I've played in it, to be outrageously funny sometimes, and funnily outrageous, of course.

MICHAEL ASPEL:

And here's Donald Sinden who immortalized Malvolio.

DONALD SINDEN:

I always like to know what I'm going to look like when I go on the stage, and I found during rehearsals that my face took on the muscular characteristics of the character. My mouth began to turn down at the edges, my eyebrows sort of elevated in the middle in a look of disdain, because he is disdainful of everybody. I take a lot of my faces from art galleries. I knew I'd seen the face that I wanted for Malvolio somewhere in a gallery. And it clicked into place one day as my computers got to work and, of course, it was the Graham Sutherland portrait of Somerset Maugham which hangs in the Tate. Off I went to get a postcard of it and there was exactly my make-up, absolutely perfect. It's a very yellow portrait and, I thought, that gave me an added dimension. When one studies Malvolio, there's nothing that he actually says that is funny. He makes no jokes. People laugh *at*

him, so it was my work as an actor to tell the audience that they
are permitted to laugh as much as they like at me.

MICHAEL ASPEL:

So we have the two households – Olivia's and Orsino's – and
Viola is the go-between.

EILEEN ATKINS:

Viola is dressed as a boy and has been sent by Orsino, whom she's
in love with, to woo Olivia, as they did in those days – send somebody to woo for them. Mind you, we do that today too, don't
we? You say to your best friend, or not even your best friend,
'Look, do you know so-and-so, well I really do like him an
awful lot, you couldn't say something for me, could you?' It's
the same kind of thing only they just did it rather more formally.
So, dressed as a boy, she goes and greets Olivia. And Olivia says,
'I really don't want to know anything about Orsino – he just
bores the pants off me.' Viola says, 'If I did love you in my
master's flame,/With such a suffering, such a deadly life,/In
your denial I would find no sense;' – because Viola herself is
utterly in love with Orsino, therefore she doesn't understand
anybody not being. Do you ever understand anybody who
doesn't think the man you're in love with is the most beautiful
thing on earth? And she says, 'I would not understand it.' She
says it with such passion, that Olivia turns to her and says,
suddenly very surprised – it's the first time you catch Olivia's
attention in the play – 'Why, what would you?' And Viola says:

> Make me a willow cabin at your gate,
> And call upon my soul within the house;
> Write loyal cantons of contemnèd love,
> And sing them loud even in the dead of night;
> Hallow your name to the reverberate hills
> And make the babbling gossip of the air
> Cry out 'Olivia!' O, you should not rest
> Between the elements of air and earth,
> But you should pity me.

(I. 5. 257–65)

For myself, I can't think of anything more absolute for one to say if one was in love. I mean, if you're in love with someone, that is exactly what you want to do. You want to go and lie down at their gate, and call their name.

MICHAEL ASPEL:

Yes. And so Viola goes on her way back to Orsino . . . but something rather strange happens. Malvolio runs after her and delivers a ring which, he says, she gave to Olivia. Malvolio leaves Viola alone on stage and she makes a speech. It's just the sort of speech that comes up in your context questions, with a comment like this: 'What is revealed about the plot complications in this soliloquy?' Soliloquy is a word that could cause panic.

JANET SUZMAN:

All it really means is a private conversation of the actor with the audience. It's simply the playwright saying to the audience, 'Look, I have this problem, let's share it', which is precisely what soliloquies do. Nobody else is on the stage, the actor is by himself. He is in a relationship of great intimacy with the audience, at least he should be, and ideally, speaking in the ideal theatre, he shouldn't even have to shout it. He should be able to just speak his thoughts.

MICHAEL ASPEL:

And so when Malvolio leaves Viola alone with the ring, she does just that.

> VIOLA:
> I left no ring with her: what means this lady?
> Fortune forbid my outside have not charmed her!
> She made good view of me, indeed so much,
> That – methought – her eyes had lost her tongue,
> For she did speak in starts, distractedly.
> She loves me, sure, the cunning of her passion
> Invites me in this churlish messenger.
> None of my lord's ring? Why, he sent her none.

I am the man! If it be so – as 'tis –
Poor lady, she were better love a dream.
                                        (II. 2. 17–26)

MICHAEL ASPEL:

Olivia's love has to be a hopeless one, but that doesn't make it unbelievable. People do fall in love at first sight, even Viola did. And the next time we see her, Viola is talking about love – man to man – with Orsino. Orsino wants to know all about a love affair that Cesario's sister once had; poor Viola is really talking about herself.

JUDI DENCH:

Viola says:

> A blank, my lord. She never told her love,
> But let concealment, like a worm i' the bud,
> Feed on her damask cheek. She pined in thought,
> And with a green and yellow melancholy,
> She sat like Patience on a monument,
> Smiling at grief. Was not this love indeed?
>   (II. 4. 109–14)

This poor little girl, who thinks she's lost her brother and thinks she's totally on her own, suddenly finds herself in love and not able to do anything about it. That speech is not a speech on its own, it's full of context when you know it. It should be very heartbreaking, I think.

JOHN BARTON:

One is touched and stirred by Viola's love for Orsino – one may think that Orsino isn't worth it but one can still be touched by the love. As a general remark, I think it's in Chekhov's *Three Sisters* that one of the characters says, 'What a lot of love about', and I think that's true of *Twelfth Night*. The whole play deals with situations of people in love; sometimes it laughs at them, and sometimes it cherishes that love, celebrates it. It does all the different things that any of us may do if we look at somebody in love – we may mock, we may sympathize, we may identify with it – all those things happen. A typical possible exam question about *Twelfth Night* is something on the lines of: 'Is Malvolio the only character who is sick of self-love in the play?' I think you could argue that there's something of self-love in Orsino's love, or perhaps he's in love with being in love. There's something self-congratulatory about his expressions of love, about how perfect and fine his love is. He's not as stupid as Malvolio but in a way he's as deluded and seduced by the romance of being in love with love.

MICHAEL ASPEL:

Let's go back to Olivia's court and witness love at its most ludicrous. Malvolio is in love with his mistress, or perhaps with her social position. There's a lot of to-ing and fro-ing in this play and, as if having two courts isn't enough, there is an extra complication to the plot. Every now and again, when no one else is on stage, a man called Sebastian rushes across it, attended by his servant, Antonio. Like Viola, these two have been shipwrecked on Illyria – and Sebastian looks just like Viola in her boy's clothing. He is, believe it or not, her twin brother who believes her drowned, just as she thought he was dead. So Shakespeare does have a lot of characters to move about, and it does make it a confusing play to read. This is something that John Cleese finds annoying.

JOHN CLEESE:

My main complaint about the play is that I think it's a fairly sloppy bit of writing, in that most of the things have not been worked out properly. I suspect that Shakespeare wrote it in a bit of a hurry and never got round to doing the second draft. For example, if you look at Malvolio, they do actually give him a terribly hard time. As someone who's done a lot of pretty hard comedy himself, it may mean something if I say that I began to feel quite sorry for Malvolio some time before the end.

MICHAEL ASPEL:

Yes, they're very cruel to him but then he's not exactly charming to them. One night Sir Toby and his friends are having a party – they're roaring drunk. Malvolio bursts in and orders them to be silent.

JOHN CLEESE:

As a result of this, they decide to get him, and they write the letter. The next thing we see is that Malvolio is wandering around, already having fantasies about marrying Olivia and being a person of great estate. It seems to me a very great weakness of the play, if they're trying to kid him with this letter into thinking that Olivia is in love with him, that he should walk on just before he finds the letter and we should suddenly discover that he is 75 per cent of the way to being hooked anyway. He picks the letter up and reads it, and seems strangely confused because Malvolio, if you're going to score off him at all, has got to be a snob but not too stupid a snob.

JOHN BARTON:

I don't quite understand what you mean. I don't think it lessens the fun in any way.

MICHAEL ASPEL:

John Barton is a formidable opponent for John Cleese because he directed *Twelfth Night* for the Royal Shakespeare Company when Donald Sinden played Malvolio.

JOHN BARTON:

I think that unless he's liable to be gulled, to be deceived by the information that Olivia is in love with him, the letter's not going to work anyway.

MICHAEL ASPEL:

Two points of view. What do you think?

JOHN CLEESE:

Malvolio reads, 'Remember who commended thy yellow stockings', and yet we learn a couple of pages later on, from Maria, that in fact Olivia can't stand the colour yellow, she hates it. Now Malvolio has been Olivia's steward for apparently quite a long time. So first of all, doesn't he have any idea what colours she likes or does not like, and secondly, just because he reads in a letter that apparently once Olivia commended 'thy yellow stockings', why should he suddenly believe it in this way? There's so much confusion going on in Malvolio's mind, that it seems to me really to weaken both him as a character and to weaken the strength of the comedy.

DONALD SINDEN:

I'm afraid I disagree with John Cleese who talks about inconsistencies in the plot. I find from Malvolio's point of view no inconsistencies whatsoever. If you're talking about the cross-gartering and the yellow stockings, can you not imagine the wonderful scene that took place, possibly a year ago, when Malvolio came in with a couple of footmen to serve the tea one day when Olivia had a lot of girlfriends there? He came in wearing yellow stockings and cross-gartered. All the girls looked at him with incredulous horror but Olivia, of course, knows him well enough and said, 'Like your yellow stockings, Malvolio, very nice.' And he said, 'Thank you, madam, thank you', and went out, taking it as a great compliment. Of course, the moment he left the room, all the girls broke up in giggles.

MICHAEL ASPEL:

That sounds lovely – has it silenced your doubts about the plot? Sir Andrew gets very jealous of Viola because Olivia prefers a mere messenger to Sir Andrew, who is a knight. The mischievous Sir Toby eggs Andrew on to write to Viola challenging her to a duel. Meanwhile Malvolio is following the instructions of his letter. Malvolio, a man who never smiled in his life, appears before Olivia wreathed in smiles, dressed very strangely in his yellow stockings and talking in such a way that Olivia naturally, thinks he's mad. She tells Maria to look after him. And, to Maria, looking after him means locking him up and teasing him unmercifully. But this isn't all. Every so often Sebastian, Viola's twin, reappears on the stage. He's going to town to have a good time with some money that his servant, Antonio, gave him. Everyone starts to confuse Sebastian and Viola. Antonio asks Viola for the money he gave Sebastian. Sir Andrew and Sir Toby get more than they bargained for from their challenge to Viola because it's Sebastian, a practised swordsman, with whom they fight. And when Olivia comes rushing out to save her Cesario from this fight, Sebastian doesn't know what's going on. But he says, 'If it be thus to dream, still let me sleep!' Sensible lad. He understands that song of Feste's which seems to hum on beneath the hilarity of the play. 'In delay there lies no plenty –/ Then come kiss me, sweet and twenty,/Youth's a stuff will not endure.' And so Olivia marries Sebastian, believing him to be Cesario. You have to remember that Sebastian can't possibly guess that he's mistaken for his own sister. He knows her under the name of Viola, and he believes she's dead. Then, for the first time in the play, Olivia and Orsino meet one another. Cesario, or Viola, comes to Olivia's house with his/her master. When Olivia calls Cesario her husband, poor Orsino is deeply shocked. But then so is Cesario/Viola because, not surprisingly, she never married Olivia. It's like a bedroom farce, without the bedrooms. You can see why the examiners sometimes ask 'whether the best comedy comes from situations where some, or all, of the people on stage do not know something the audience knows'. Even the question is confusing. And by now you're probably as confused as the cast are. So how are we going to resolve this? What we need is a teacher, and here he is, Tony O'Sullivan.

TONY O'SULLIVAN:

The climax of this comedy, the situation comedy, is beautifully resolved in Act V when, for the first time, the eagerly awaited confrontation of the two twins takes place on stage and everything can be explained without words.

MICHAEL ASPEL:

It's a magical moment when the twins are reunited and, by this magic, many marriages can be made. Viola wins her Orsino. Olivia has her Sebastian. And even Maria gets her man, Sir Toby. But someone's left out of the dancing and the celebration at the end – Malvolio. He has no place in this party.

DONALD SINDEN:

It's like a five-year-old child saying: 'I'll be revenged on the whole pack of you.'

MICHAEL ASPEL:

This is a very dark moment for the last minutes of a comedy. Throughout this play Shakespeare introduces sad and savage notes. Remember that *Twelfth Night* is the last in the long festive season of Christmas; the time to celebrate is running out, tempers are fraying and it will be back to the tedium of normal life and work tomorrow. The exciting thing about this comedy is that it offers no escape from reality. It captures all that's rich and romantic, and also ridiculous.

JOHN BARTON:

Well, a comedy does not necessarily mean something that's just funny and jolly, and something that has a 'happy ever after'. There are dark comedies, or there are comedies with tragic elements, or bitter comedies, or sardonic comedies. I think the idea of a comedy just being a jolly thing has only existed at very few times in history. After all, today you get black comedies. Shakespeare wrote relatively few straight comedies. In a play like *Twelfth Night*, his sense of the realities of life tends to clash with the fairytale sense of 'happy ever after', and I'm sure this is deliberate on his part. I'm sure that only one bit of him believed in 'and they all got married and lived happily ever after'. That's the convention of comedy but the reality of life isn't like that.

TONY O'SULLIVAN:

It's quite significant that after Malvolio's slightly sour note at the end of the play we also have Feste having the last word with a song which reminds us that 'the rain it raineth every day' – in other words that the world is harsher and more cruel than we have been given to understand and there is a harsher world awaiting us.

MICHAEL ASPEL:

Yes, Shakespeare shows us that loving someone isn't always easy. Sometimes it can make you very lonely. The beauty of *Twelfth Night* is in Shakespeare's control. Cruelty never overcomes comedy but it is there in his play, as it is in life.

JOHN BARTON:

It's probably the richest of Shakespeare's comedies – the richest in variety. It's very funny, it's full of marvellous poetry, it's sad, it's savage, it's full of mood and varieties of mood. I think it's the diversity of it which makes it the richest of his comedies.

Twelfth Night and the Feast of Misrule

It is quite likely that *Twelfth Night* was so named because it was written for a first performance on Twelfth Night itself, 6 January, the final day of the twelve days of Christmas. A whole book (Leslie Hotson, *The First Night of 'Twelfth Night'*, Hart-Davis, 1954) has been written to support the case that it was in fact first performed on 6 January 1601, at the royal palace at White-hall, when Queen Elizabeth's guest of honour was an Italian duke, Don Virginio Orsino. It is known that Shakespeare's company, the Lord Chamberlain's Men, actually did perform a play after supper on that occasion, but whether *Twelfth Night* was the play is still an open question.

In any case it is a play with a holiday atmosphere, and one that would fit happily into the generous festival spirit of an Elizabethan Christmas. Eating, drinking and merry-making were the main features of that season, then as now, and in great houses there were special customs associated with the celebra-tions:

Of old ordinary course, there is always one appointed to make sport in the court, called commonly lord of misrule: whose office is not unknown to such as have been brought up in noblemen's houses and among great housekeepers which use liberal feasting in that season.

The duties of the Lord of Misrule were to preside over the festivities and feasts in the kind of large household that the historian Holinshed describes above. Sometimes he was chosen by lot, perhaps by finding a bean in his piece of Christmas cake – in which case he was known as 'The King of the Bean'. It was all part of an upside-down sort of holiday mood when, for once in the year, the youngest or least important member of a household or an institution became the most important. It's a custom that still survives in some places – in France, for instance, who ever finds the bean in their cake becomes the king for the day.

During Shakespeare's lifetime, all sorts of traditional holiday customs, including the goings-on presided over by the Lord of

26. *Malvolio accosts Viola – Laurence Olivier and Vivien Leigh in the Shakespeare Memorial Theatre Company production in 1955.*

27. *Viola's duel with Sir Andrew. Diana Rigg and David Warner in the production by the Royal Shakespeare Company, 1966.*

28. Sir Andrew Aguecheek and Sir Toby Belch. Royal Shakespeare Company, 1979.

29. *Feste. Royal Shakespeare Company, 1979*

30. *'One face, one voice, one habit, and two persons!' Viola and Sebastian meet.*
Royal Shakespeare Company, 1970.

31. 'By my life, this is my lady's hand.' Malvolio (Donald Sinden) finds the letter. Royal Shakespeare Company,

Misrule, were consistently attacked by Puritan preachers and writers. It is clear from *Twelfth Night* itself that the term 'Puritan' was often used to mean little more than 'killjoy'. In the play it is Malvolio who is briefly compared with the Puritans, and it is he who does his best to dampen the holiday spirit; refusing to laugh at Feste's jokes, and breaking up Sir Toby's midnight party. It is because of his intolerant disapproval of the fun that everyone else is having that he becomes the butt of the comic plot. Everyone in Olivia's household, including (usually) Olivia herself, goes along with the mood of leisurely ease and good living that Sir Toby Belch, above all, represents. Only Malvolio keeps up the air of stiff and moralizing disapproval that provokes Sir Toby's outburst: 'Dost thou think, because thou art virtuous, there shall be no more cakes and ale?' *Twelfth Night* is a play that is full of a 'cakes and ale' sort of atmosphere.

'Are all the people mad?'

Sebastian's reaction to Illyrian ways is understandable. People start mistaking him for Cesario/Viola as soon as he gets into town, and the confusions that follow are not resolved until the final scene. But madness, especially that variety of it which is called love, is certainly a feature of life in Illyria.

Madness was often thought of in Shakespeare's time as 'possession' – being possessed by devils or spirits. In *Twelfth Night* madness and love, possession and obsession, are often equated. Orsino and Olivia suffer from two different kinds of love-madness. Orsino's swooning, obsessive adoration of an unobtainable lady has become a cult rather than the more normal love. He feeds his love with music and with flowers:

> Away before me to sweet beds of flowers!
> Love thoughts lie rich when canopied with bowers.
> (I. 1. 41-2)

Olivia's love for Cesario/Viola is love at first sight, and it hits her like a thunderbolt. ('Even so quickly may one catch the plague?') Her total capitulation is all the funnier because of all the vows of chastity and mourning that she had made after her brother's death. This cult of her brother's memory parallels, at the beginning of the play, Orsino's cult of her; both are cut through by the plot.

The play's most ludicrous lover is Malvolio. His love for Olivia is the most thoroughly mocked *within* the play, for it makes him vulnerable to Maria's trick at his expense. The root of his love is ambition and self-seeking; his amorous fantasies, overheard by Sir Toby and his friends, all have to do with lording it over people. Yellow-stockinged, cross-gartered, and smiling madly, Malvolio is a sort of caricature of the idiocies of love.

The truest lover in *Twelfth Night*, Viola, is also the most silent. Because of her disguise she cannot give direct expression to her love, but hints at it in oblique references:

> She never told her love,
> But let concealment, like a worm i' the bud,
> Feed on her damask cheek. She pined in thought,
> And with a green and yellow melancholy,
> She sat like Patience on a monument,
> Smiling at grief. Was not this love indeed?
>
> (II. 4. 109-14)

Twins and transvestism

Shakespeare had used identical twins as the mainspring of a plot before – indeed, in *The Comedy of Errors* he used *two* pairs – but before *Twelfth Night* he never explored the comic possibilities of using identical twins of opposite sexes. Although it's a genetic impossibility, it's a device that Shakespeare puts to very good comic effect, and combined with Viola's adoption of a male disguise it carries the play forward on a constant wave of laughter. In the first part of the play the laughs are all at Viola's embarrassment as she has to cope with the results of her disguise, first Olivia's falling in love with her, and then the hostility of Sir Toby and Sir Andrew. In the second part of the play the laughs come from Sebastian's bewilderment as he tries to make sense of the situations that his resemblance to Viola/Cesario plunges him into.

Twelfth Night is a festive play. We still have pantomimes that turn reality upside down to make us laugh. They are just as popular as they always were, and they use many of the kinds of comic devices that are found in Shakespeare's plots. Transvestism, in particular, is a feature of pantomime. The pantomime dame is usually a male comic in skirts, and the principal boy is traditionally a pretty girl in male disguise, just like Viola.

But of course, in the Elizabethan theatre the position was even more complicated than that. What Shakespeare's first audiences were actually watching, when they followed the fortunes of Viola/Cesario, was a boy actor, pretending to be a girl dressed up as a boy. The thoroughly topsy-turvy nature of the situation must have added to the theatrical joke.

Feste and the songs

We know something about some of the actors who were part of Shakespeare's company, and it seems fairly clear that, when he was creating a character, Shakespeare often took into account the style and range of the actor who was going to play the part. The character of Feste in *Twelfth Night* has a lot in common with that of the Fool in *King Lear* and that of Touchstone, the fool in *As You Like It*. It seems likely that these parts were written with a particular player in mind, and evidence suggests that it was the actor Robert Armin. About Armin himself not very much is known. He joined Shakespeare's company, who were then known as the Lord Chamberlain's Men, in 1599, and had been a member of another company before that. He went on to write plays himself, as well as a book about fools and jesters called *Foole upon Foole*. He must have had a good voice, because the characters he played are often given songs to sing. He was obviously not a broad comedian, but a very subtle artist, whose humour could be bitter, wise or touched with melancholy.

Feste is a good example of this type of fool. He is slightly detached from the other comic characters. His position socially seems to be less restricted, since he appears both in Orsino's court and in Olivia's household, the only one of the characters, apart from Viola the messenger, to move freely between these two worlds. 'Foolery, sir,' he explains to Cesario/Viola, 'does walk about the orb like the sun, it shines everywhere.' He uses his wit to avoid giving a straight answer to anyone about his movements.

The songs he is given to sing are an important part of the play. From Orsino's opening lines to the epilogue song, the play is accompanied by music.

'Come away Death', the song Feste sings for Orsino, is very appropriate to the mood of hopeless love that is cultivated in Orsino's court. The song is beautiful, and heavy with self-indulgence and self-pity.

'O Mistress Mine', the song he sings for Sir Toby and Sir Andrew in Olivia's house, is a delightful, slightly poignant love song on the 'Gather ye rosebuds while ye may' theme. Some writers have suggested that the mistress in the song is meant to recall the mistress of the house, Olivia, and that the song is an appeal to her to break her vow and marry.

Feste has sometimes been played as an ageing man, and there are certainly references in the play to the possibility that he is going out of favour as he gets older. In the first exchange between Feste and Maria she warns him that Olivia is angry with him and that he is risking being 'turned away' or sacked. The last song of all in the play has sometimes been staged as if Feste has indeed been turned away, so that, while the lovers enter the house to prepare for the marriage of Orsino and Viola, he is left out in 'the wind and the rain'. The epilogue song may, in other words, mean a little or a lot. One commentator has seen in it the life story of a lecherous drunkard, a sort of rake's progress. The final verse is a conventional epilogue, the players' apology and a reminder that it is only a play that we have been watching.

When that I was and a lit-tle ti-ny boy, With a
hey - ho, the wind — and the rain, A fool - ish thing was
but — a — toy, For the rain it rain - eth
ev - 'ry — day, With a hey - ho, the
wind and the rain, For the rain it rain - eth ev - 'ry — day.

'What country, friends, is this?'

Where was Illyria? Here are some of the suggestions that have been put forward:

Shakespeare seems to have thought of Illyria as a semi-independent fief of the Holy Roman Empire, like the contemporary Dutch Indes.

(John W. Draper, 1948)

We are here in fairyland; why should we try to discover the real nature of the personages? They are children of the imagination.

(E. Montegut, 1867)

The scene is laid in Illyria, whilst the names of the Dramatis Personae are a mixture of Spanish, Italian and English. The best mode of reconciling the discrepancies arising from so many conflicting circumstances appears to be the assumption, first, that Duke Orsino is a Venetian governor of that portion of Dalmatia which was all of ancient Illyria remaining under the dominion of the republic at the commencement of the seventeenth century, and that his attendants, Valentine, Curio, etc., as well as Olivia, Malvolio, and Maria, are also Venetians; and secondly, that Sir Toby and Sir Andrew are English residents; the former a maternal uncle to Olivia – her father, a Venetian Count, having married Sir Toby's sister.

(Joseph Knight, 1884)

Illyria is obviously a land of love, music, and leisure ... it might be English, Italian, French, Russian (before the revolution) or, with some adaptation, American or Utopian; medieval, renaissance or modern.

(John Russell Brown, 1957)

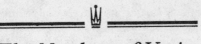

The Merchant of Venice

(in order of appearance)

Michael Aspel	*presenter*
Judi Dench	*actress*
Timothy West	*actor*
Janet Suzman	*actress*
Jonathan Miller	*director*
Roy Blachford	*teacher*
Joan Plowright	*actress*
Jon Finch	*actor*

MICHAEL ASPEL:

This set book takes us to Italy, to the city of Venice, where Shakespeare stages his only commercial comedy. It's *The Merchant of Venice*, in which we follow the fortunes of Shylock, the Jewish money-lender, and we share in the prosperity of Portia, a rich young lady who lives in the suburbs of Venice at Belmont. It's one of Shakespeare's most well-known but not necessarily best-loved plays.

JUDI DENCH:

I didn't ever want to do the play and I gave in, in a very weak moment, to play Portia. The nice thing was that my husband was playing Bassanio – that was very nice. I don't like any of the characters. I think they all behave appallingly.

TIMOTHY WEST:

It's a slightly mucky play, I think. I've never been happy in it.

JANET SUZMAN:

I know in my heart that it's a marvellous play but I think it's a desperately difficult one. Shakespeare's style seems to change. He moves from highly classical, very overwrought conceits to ordinary phrases in the flick of a switch, and that means it's rather difficult for the actors to get hold of consistently warm characters.

MICHAEL ASPEL:

Jonathan Miller could cope. He set his production of *The Merchant of Venice* in the nineteenth century, where Shylock was just a banker and Portia an early example of women's lib. Interesting how you can really muck about with Shakespeare – change the century, alter the clothes and the sets – he doesn't seem to mind. But Jonathan Miller recognized the fact that the characters are less interesting in this play than the ideas and the structure.

JONATHAN MILLER:

It has a most fantastic internal symmetry. Beautiful oppositions and conflicts are presented and resolved.

MICHAEL ASPEL:

It's a play in which there are two separate plots: the bond plot, where Shylock lends three thousand ducats to Antonio, and the casket caper, where Portia can only marry the man astute enough to pick the right casket. If he finds the right box, he wins her picture and he takes her money. It is a love story but not a particularly tender one. Love is seen to grow when there's money in the bank. The heart is the deposit account.

ROY BLACHFORD:

Jonathan Miller is right when he talks about the intricacy of the different plots – how the casket plot and the bond plot are very tightly interwoven. On the stage it makes for tremendous drama. This symmetry of plot, which is often talked about, really is a critic's dream.

MICHAEL ASPEL:

It could be your nightmare if you haven't given it any thought by June, when you might be asked to show 'how the minor characters and episodes of the play mirror the important events.' It's a play full of reflections of its own theme. Have you noticed how the scene with the clown figure, Launcelot Gobbo, and his old father makes a comic parallel with the more heavy relationship of Shylock and his daughter, Jessica?

ROY BLACHFORD:

The play opens with Antonio and Bassanio talking about their fortunes. Antonio is a man who has invested quite heavily in the sea, in merchandise, and obviously at this point we realize that if the sea fails him, if there are storms, the ships will founder and he will lose all his money.

MICHAEL ASPEL:

And that's no idle plot complication – he will lose it all, just because young Bassanio wanted him to raise three thousand ducats on the surety of those ships so he could go to Belmont and woo Portia. What sort of man is Bassanio? Here's Joan Plowright who was Jonathan Miller's Portia.

JOAN PLOWRIGHT:

He is a bit of a gigolo. When he first tells Antonio why he wants money to go and court this lady, his first line is: 'In Belmont is a lady richly left', and his next remark is 'and she is fair'. But his first consideration is the fact that she's got money.

ROY BLACHFORD:

Now in the second scene we meet Portia and we see at once that she's looking for a suitor.

JOAN PLOWRIGHT:

She's got money. She's therefore in the market for a lot of gentlemen who are rich, but not perhaps very attractive. She makes snide remarks about them all to her maid. She's very witty. She doesn't take any of them seriously except for Bassanio, of course, whom she's obviously fallen madly in love with.

JANET SUZMAN:

I think that one of the loveliest things one must realize about Shakespeare is that when his lovers fall in love, boom, they fall in love, no questions asked.

MICHAEL ASPEL:

If you look closely at that list of suitors Portia mocks so wittily, you might find she does it less than prettily. What she objects to is the *foreignness* of them all, except for Bassanio who is one of her own kind. Now is Portia giving way to prejudice? Is it a coincidence that immediately after this scene we meet the most alien of characters – Shylock, the Jew, the moneylender?

JONATHAN MILLER:

In the sixteenth century the character of the Jew was more or less identified with the traditional figure of the morality play devil. He was simply a stereotype of evil. I don't think that Shakespeare represents him in this way, although that's often the way in which he's been performed on the stage. Nor is he merely a figure of pathos either, which is the other extreme to which one can go.

One has to try to set him in some realistic social context so that his behaviour becomes credible and the behaviour of others towards him becomes credible. Now this of course is possible in the nineteenth century but it's much harder to understand the role of the Jew in the sixteenth century because you have to bring to it all sorts of expert historical knowledge about what Jews were like and what sort of life they led, either in England or in Venice. And that's very difficult. Whereas in the nineteenth century you can make the figure of the Jew much more readily identifiable – his behaviour, his tendencies and so forth. You can simply make him a wealthy banker who lends money, which is all bankers do, so one hasn't got to distinguish a moneylender as something vicious, any more than a bank that offers an overdraft and charges interest on it which is all that he's doing.

And in fact then the play becomes rather intriguing. If he's not distinguishable from every one else except because they're prejudiced against him, and if their prejudice against him is all that distinguishes him, then their unpleasant behaviour to him becomes a study of prejudice rather than simply the reaction of a virtuous community towards an evil individual. And it's quite clear from what Shakespeare does that he doesn't intend him to be an evil individual – he's a person who reacts to all sorts of complicated social stresses.

JOAN PLOWRIGHT:

To be an outsider creates enormous resentment, finally possibly hatred, and quite justifiably so. I mean any oppressed minority today feels the same. And so one treats Shylock as that – he is part of an oppressed minority who makes a jokey bond, a pound of your flesh.

ROY BLACHFORD:

An interesting question, perhaps, to ask yourselves is: 'Who exactly is the merchant of Venice?' Quite clearly, Antonio is principally meant to be the merchant, but Shylock, of course, is a usurer, a money-lender; he is a merchant of sorts in Venice. And the way Bassanio treats his whole wooing of Portia – he sees winning Portia's love very much in terms of possessions, of ownership, of wealth. He wants to win her for her fortune.

MICHAEL ASPEL:

There are a great number of references to love as wealth, a kind of merchandise. While we wait for the three-month period of Shylock's bond with Antonio to expire, we fill in the time with love stories where the worth of the girl is weighed against the gold she brings with her. The scene darts back and forth between Belmont and Venice, between the caskets and the cash-register of Shylock's home. One night Jessica defects to the 'Christians with varnished faces'. She elopes with Lorenzo, a friend of Bassanio's and Antonio's, the very people who have oppressed her father, Shylock.

JONATHAN MILLER:

It's very, very interesting the way he talks about the loss of his daughter and the way in which he wishes a pound of flesh in return, because he actually talks about Jessica being his own flesh.

JANET SUZMAN:

There's a brave girl. I mean can you imagine escaping from your over-loving, paternal, patriarchal daddy the way she does.

JONATHAN MILLER:

Shakespeare has a curious, sort of triangular obsession with daughters who owe loyalty both to their fathers and to their lovers.

MICHAEL ASPEL:

It does seem as if Shakespeare was still working this idea out in his imagination. You may have spotted the problem in *Romeo and Juliet*, and in *A Midsummer Night's Dream*. It's that old saying that 'every marriage makes a father weep' which worries Shakespeare, especially when he wrote comedies where everyone has to make up by the end of the play. It's interesting that these opposing claims of father and lover, so untidy in this play, are dealt with on a grander scale and resolved quite beautifully in a later play, a tragedy in fact, *King Lear*. In a sense Portia is also caught between father and lover – there's no grip stronger than the will of a dead father. While Shylock laments the loss of his daughter, Portia's suitors undergo trial by casket. It's a serious moment. Portia must marry if the choice is correct. As for the man, if he chooses wrongly, he has sworn never to woo another woman. The Princes of Morocco and Arragon, in turn, go for gold and silver, dazzled by the glitter and by the inscriptions on the box: '*Who chooseth me shall gain what many men desire*', and '*Who chooseth me shall get as much as he deserves*'. Their failure leaves the way open for Bassanio's success. Has Roy Blachford any suggestions on why Bassanio should be the lucky one?

ROY BLACHFORD:

'*Who chooseth me must give and hazard all he hath.*' The words '*hazard all he hath*' tie in rather well with all that's gone before – Bassanio has hazarded everything for Portia's love and he equally has asked his friend, Antonio, to hazard all that he hath.

MICHAEL ASPEL:

The moment of Bassanio's choice is played out with pageantry and with song.

> SONG
> Tell me where is fancy bred,
> Or in the heart, or in the head?
> How begot, how nourished?
> Reply, reply.
>
> It is engendered in the eyes,
> With gazing fed, and fancy dies
> In the cradle where it lies.
> Let us all ring fancy's knell.
> I'll begin it – Ding, dong, bell.
>   (III. 2. 63–71)

JON FINCH:

Then Bassanio says:

> So may the outward shows be least themselves.
> The world is still deceived with ornament.
> In law, what plea so tainted and corrupt,
> But being seasoned with a gracious voice,
> Obscures the show of evil? In religion,
> What damnèd error but some sober brow
> Will bless it and approve it with a text,
> Hiding the grossness with fair ornament?
> There is no vice so simple but assumes
> Some mark of virtue on his outward parts.
>   (III. 2. 73–82)

It does pertain, you know, to all of us. The idea that ornament and money are the outward show of success. This is why Bassanio wins in the casket scene. The two guys who go before make mistakes, and he goes for lead. He thinks that is where the real worth of the world and the real worth of this particular lady lies. The outward show doesn't mean anything to him. But he's worked it out – it's rather like a crossword puzzle.

TIMOTHY WEST:

It could be said that this was one of Shakespeare's less subtle ideas – that it should be quite clear to anybody who understood Portia's particular sort of sensibilities that the one to go for was the cheap one.

JOAN PLOWRIGHT:

Portia, for the first time, seems to be totally real and expressing all the emotions of a woman very deeply in love.

> You see me, Lord Bassanio, where I stand,
> Such as I am. Though for myself alone
> I would not be ambitious in my wish
> To wish myself much better, yet for you
> I would be trebled twenty times myself,
> A thousand times more fair, ten thousand times
> More rich that only to stand high in your account,
> I might in virtues, beauties, livings, friends,
> Exceed account; but the full sum of me
> Is sum of something, which to term in gross,
> Is an unlessoned girl, unschooled, unpractisèd,
> Happy in this, she is not yet so old
> But she may learn; happier than this,
> She is not bred so dull but she can learn;
> Happiest of all is that her gentle spirit
> Commits itself to yours to be directed,
> As from her lord, her governor, her king.
> Myself and what is mine to you and yours
> Is now converted. But now I was the lord
> Of this fair mansion, master of my servants,
> Queen o'er myself; and even now, but now,
> This house, these servants, and this same myself
> Are yours, my lord's. I give them with this ring,

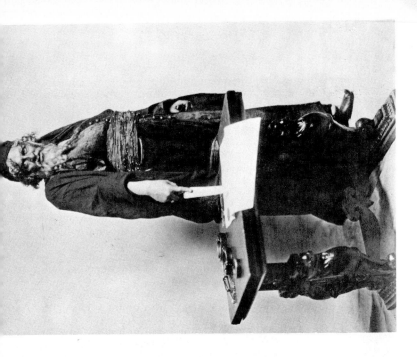

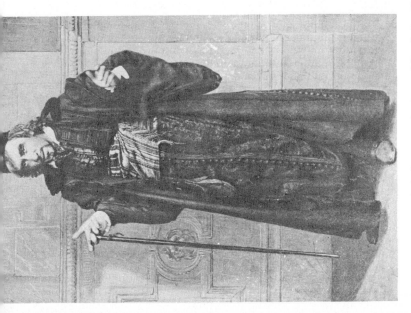

32, 33: *Two earlier Shylocks, Henry Irving and Beerbohm Tree.*

35. *Shylock in his counting house, watched by Jessica.
Royal Shakespeare Company, The Other Place, 1978.*

36. *'This bond doth give thee here no jot of blood.' Portia
(Judi Dench) interrupts Shylock (Emrys James). Royal
Shakespeare Company, 1971.*

37. *The Prince of Morocco chooses the gold casket. Questors, 1977.*

38. *The court room. Royal Shakespeare Company, 1971.*

Which when you part from, lose, or give away,
Let it presage the ruin of your love,
And be my vantage to exclaim on you.

(III. 2. 149–74)

MICHAEL ASPEL:

It's a beautiful speech and the whole scene is enchanted. The lover's kiss has awoken the princess from her father's possessive spell. But you'll need to be wide awake because it's a scene that's often appeared in your context questions with such comments as: (a) What promise does Bassanio make when he is given the ring? (b) Explain briefly why this promise is broken. The answer lies in the court scene.

ROY BLACHFORD:

Portia and Bassanio, of course, are now contracted but, before they can be married, news comes along – a letter brought by Jessica and Lorenzo from Venice to say that Antonio's ships have foundered, he's lost his fortune. And of course this means that the play will have to return to Venice so that Antonio can meet his bond. Portia, being the lady that she is, immediately feels bound to her husband-to-be and decides on a plan of action to help Bassanio and his best friend, Antonio.

JANET SUZMAN:

Why on earth does this rather quietly brought-up, rich 'gel' loose herself into Venice and dress up as a young lawyer? Well, she's a funny girl. She combines a tremendous *Harper's and Queen* distance, and she also obviously enjoys the fun of pretending to be somebody else and testing her love.

JOAN PLOWRIGHT:

That would be the sort of woman who could disguise herself as a man and go to court. Obviously she'd been seething all her life at the fact that none of her potential had been recognized – that she had a good mind and wasn't able to use it; that she could function in a man's world; and, as she proves in *The Merchant of*

Venice, she can function much better than a man. She's the one who wins the trial scene.

MICHAEL ASPEL:

But did Shylock have a chance in the hostile atmosphere of a Christian court? The invective against him punctuates this scene; 'Jew dog' and 'devil' are used almost as evidence. So what was Shakespeare's intention?

ROY BLACHFORD:

He really denies the citizens of Venice any common humanity. He makes them say things to Shylock, treating Shylock as though he were a creature of another species, as someone of infinitely lower importance in society than they are. Much in the same way that the Nazis treated the Jews in pre-war Germany. So Shylock stands alone in court. There's no one else there to plead his case.

JONATHAN MILLER:

And he gives a wonderful speech about the nature of irrational dislike when he says, 'Some men there are love not a gaping pig,/ Some that are mad if they behold a cat', and the extraordinary thing about people who can't hold their water if they hear a bagpipe play. It's marvellously witty and ironic, and no one else in the play speaks with so much irony or intelligence.

ROY BLACHFORD:

Are we to see him as more sinned against than sinning? Or are we to see him as a Jew, a villain, an evil man?

JONATHAN MILLER:

Well, I think that there is one sense in which Shakespeare intends us to see Shylock as evil, and it's the sense in which Shakespeare is an Englishman of the sixteenth century for whom the Jew was necessarily evil, as being a representative of the race that killed Christ. And therefore he is meant to bear the blood of Christ on his head. In that sense I think Shakespeare is a man of his own times, and we have to sympathize with Shakespeare in that respect and see that the Jew is being seen as a type rather than a person. That doesn't mean that Shakespeare is being anti-semitic; it means that Shakespeare is simply being a Christian creature of the sixteenth century. But Shakespeare, as a person who could never suppress his human interest, found it impossible to write a two-dimensional type and, although in fact Shylock in some respects behaves in an automatically evil way, in showing no mercy for example, and in being flintily resistant to any sort of appeal to his better nature, nevertheless we do see him as a three-dimensional character.

ROY BLACHFORD:

So Shylock is the vulnerable figure at the end, the lonely figure in the middle of the stage. And Portia gives the speech in which she asks Shylock to show some mercy.

JONATHAN MILLER:

Portia has said: 'Then must the Jew be merciful', and the speech is given in response to Shylock's obstinate question: 'On what compulsion must I? Tell me that.' So her reply comes, I think, with an air of impatience rather than nobility, whereas usually what happens is that the audience draws in its breath and sits back for a cello sonata from Portia. But in fact what she says is, 'The quality of mercy is not *strained*', and she makes the point to someone who has failed to understand it.

ROY BLACHFORD:

He doesn't understand Portia's speech – Portia is bending over backwards to say to Shylock 'Do show some mercy' – and all he can say is 'I crave the law'. But because he has shown no mercy, because he cannot understand what the Christian Portia has said to him, we must go against him; we do not sympathize with him.

MICHAEL ASPEL:

And we don't see him again. The bond story is over, the caskets all opened. But the play isn't finished. There's a third plot – the ring plot. The disguised Portia beguiles Bassanio to give her the ring she gave him earlier in payment for legal services. And later back in Belmont there's no way she's going to resume wifely duties until the ring has reappeared on Bassanio's finger. Her maid, Nerissa, dressed up as her boy clerk, has pulled the same trick on her husband, Gratiano. Jessica and Lorenzo seem to be enjoying their honeymoon rather more – they have a long, poetic love scene. But in the end Portia and Nerissa tell the truth and all is happy ever after. Your examiners have enjoyed the ending, because in the past they have wanted you to show how, after the tension of the trial scene, Shakespeare uses (a) Lorenzo and Jessica and (b) the episode of the rings, to create a mood of happiness in which the play can end. Do our three Portias – Judi Dench, Joan Plowright and Janet Suzman – find these scenes happy and funny?

JUDI DENCH:

They go home and then, when you think it's going to be all right, she does all that terrible teasing. That's not very funny. Jessica, she runs away from her dad and takes all his money; it's not a very nice thing to do. Hers can't be a happy marriage, can it?

JOAN PLOWRIGHT:

Listen to what Jessica says: 'In such a night/Did young Lorenzo swear he loved her well,/Stealing her soul with many vows of faith,/And ne'er a true one.' And he accuses her. He says, 'In such a night/Did Jessica steal from the wealthy Jew,/And with an unthrift love did run from Venice/As far as Belmont.' So, in other words, Lorenzo could be thinking, 'If she did that to her father, she might do something similar to me.'

JANET SUZMAN:

I think that scene is very sweet between the two of them: 'Sit, Jessica. Look how the floor of heaven/Is thick inlaid with patens of bright gold.' It's a sweet scene.

MICHAEL ASPEL:

A sweet moment, perhaps, in what does seem to be a pretty sour play. But *The Merchant of Venice* is an interesting one in which Shakespeare has explored complicated ideas about what people owe one another as parents, as children, as friends and lovers. It's telling that the play in which many oaths have been broken ends with another oath: 'Well, while I live I'll fear no other thing/So sore as keeping safe Nerissa's ring.'

JUDI DENCH:

Now a question I have seen asked is this: ' "The women in *The Merchant of Venice* are more sensible, more honest and much nicer than the men." What is your opinion?' Well, this might take me a couple of days to answer. I don't think anybody in *The Merchant of Venice* is very nice – I think they're all absolutely awful. They're so awful to Shylock and Shylock's really so beastly to them. He's not got much compassion for anybody, Shylock. It's no good saying, 'Well, he's badly treated; he ought to have his pound of flesh.' He wants to kill somebody. Then we have got Bassanio. Well, I don't know. Is he after the money, I wonder? I don't know, maybe not; maybe he really is fond of her. Portia – all that terrible bit about the ring at the end. I'm surprised at the play, really. I'm surprised at Shakespeare having written it.

Shakespeare's sources

A number of traditional stories had told of the 'flesh-bond' that is the central feature of the plot of *The Merchant of Venice*. But the version of the story that is closest to Shakespeare's play comes in a collection of Italian tales called *Il Pecorone*, which was published in Milan in 1558. Here is a summary of the plot:

Giannetto is the godson of Ansaldo, a rich merchant of Venice. His indulgent godfather equips a fine trading ship for Giannetto, who sails off to see the world. But after a few days he comes to the harbour of Belmonte where there is a palace belonging to a rich widow. He is told that the first man who succeeds in making love to the Lady of Belmonte will be able to marry her and become the lord of the country; suitors who fail, however, lose their ships and all their goods in forfeit. Giannetto decides to put into the harbour and try to win the Lady. That night she drugs him (as she does all her suitors) and so he forfeits his ship with all its cargo. He is obliged to return to Venice empty-handed. The next year Ansaldo finds enough money to allow Giannetto to put to sea again, but Giannetto only gets as far as Belmonte, where he again loses everything to the Lady. Ansaldo is now poor, but the following year, when Giannetto insists that he wants to go and try to seek his fortune at sea again, Ansaldo raises the money for a new ship and goods by borrowing money from a Jew. A bond is made that if the money is not repaid by a certain day the Jew may take a pound of Ansaldo's flesh. Giannetto sails straight for Belmonte and this time succeeds in winning the Lady. They are married and there are general celebrations. Giannetto forgets about the bond until too late; hurrying back to Venice he finds that Ansaldo's time is up and the Jew is insisting on the penalty agreed. Meantime the Lady of Belmonte, disguised as a lawyer, arrives in Venice and is asked to judge the case. She prevents the Jew from claiming his bond by proving that he has no right to shed any of Ansaldo's blood, or to take either more or less than an exact pound of flesh from his body.

Still in disguise, she refuses Giannetto's offer of payment but asks for his ring, which he parts with unwillingly, explaining that it is a present from his wife. The Lady gets back to Belmonte some days before Giannetto returns, bringing his godfather Ansaldo. She pretends to be very angry that Giannetto has given her ring away, and accuses him of giving it to another woman. Finally she lets him into her secret. He is delighted and astonished at her story. Ansaldo is married to one of the ladies in waiting at the palace, and they all live happily ever after.

It is obvious how much Shakespeare took from this source. The fact that no English translation of the tale has ever been found suggests that he may have been able to read Italian. The changes that Shakespeare made are revealing. He showed Bassanio in a slightly better light than Giannetto; Bassanio asks Antonio for a loan only once in the play (though we do know from the text that he has borrowed from him before). He completely changed the story of the wooing of the Lady of Belmonte, by making the trial of her suitors entirely different – he took the story of the caskets from a different source, the *Gesta Romanorum*. Portia is an altogether nicer person than the original mistress of Belmont. Antonio is Bassanio's friend, rather than his godfather, and Gratiano, not Antonio, is married off to Nerissa.

The caskets plot

The caskets plot is part of the fairytale side of *The Merchant of Venice*. In the original source, the *Gesta Romanorum*, the story of the three caskets had a Christian moral – each casket had a spiritual meaning and the lead casket stood for 'a simple life and a poor, which the chosen men choose, that they may be wedded to our blessed Lord Jesu Christ by humilitie and obeysaunce'. Portia's three suitors, bold Morocco, arrogant Arragon, and Bassanio, the true lover, choose according to their natures; but the result is never really in doubt – the laws of fairytale mean that the third one to come along has got to be the winner.

However, the moral lessons of the caskets plot are reflected in the rest of the play. In the court scene, where the virtue of mercy is continually stressed against the strict rule of law, it is Shylock who finally 'gets as much as he deserves'. Antonio is the person above all others in the play who is prepared to 'give and hazard all he hath'.

Usury

Thou shalt not lend upon usury to thy brother; usury of money, usury of victuals, usury of anything that is lent upon usury: unto a stranger thou mayest lend upon usury; but unto thy brother thou shalt not lend upon usury.

(Deuteronomy 23: 19–20)

It's so normal now to pay interest on a loan that the Elizabethan attitude to usury is hard to understand. For centuries usury, the taking of interest, had been against the law in England. But by the time of Elizabeth it had come to be accepted that usury was a necessary evil. Credit was becoming a way of life; many great nobles were deeply in debt, and so was the Queen herself. The economy was changing, from feudalism to capitalism, and it was essential to be able to raise money in order to make money, especially for merchants who, like Antonio, were equipping ships to trade abroad.

Rich landowners were not content to stay on their country estates. They were flocking to London, and were either selling land or raising loans to include their appetite for the new luxury goods that increased trade was making available, and their taste for expensive city life in the rapidly growing capital. By 1615 so many noblemen were spending most of their time in London that King James issued a proclamation requiring noblemen and gentlemen to reside at their country mansions for at least nine months of the year. Property prices in London tumbled as a result.

Usury, though it was needed, was still despised. It had only just ceased to be against the law and the interest rate was still controlled by law; it was illegal to charge more than 10 per cent interest. Because Englishmen had, until recently, been prevented by their church law from lending at interest, it had been Jews and foreigners who had been the money-lenders and usurers of the society.

So usury was legal, widespread, and an essential part of the expanding economy, but it still carried a stigma. Antonio, in *The Merchant of Venice*, who 'lends out money gratis', is a model of the sort of Christian businessman that everyone felt *ought* to exist. When he and Shylock argue about the ethics of making money 'breed' they are going over a familiar debate.

There is no difference between usury, fraud, and violent robbing, as who should say, he that is a usurer is a deceitful false man, an errant thief and an extreme extortioner.

(St Jerome, c. 347–420)

The Jews were forbidden to take usury from their brethren, i.e. from other Jews. By this we are given to understand that to take usury from any man is simply evil, because we ought to treat every man as our neighbour and brother, especially in the state of the Gospel whereto we are called. They were permitted, however, to take usury from foreigners, not as though it were lawful, but in order to avoid a greater evil, lest to wit, through avarice to which they were prone, according to Isaiah, they should take usury from Jews, who were worshippers of God.

(St Thomas Aquinas, 1225–74)

For since there must be Borrowing and Lending, and men are so hard of Heart, as they will not lend freely, Usury must be permitted.

(Francis Bacon, 1561–1626)

Anti-semitism

The Merchant of Venice is a play that tends to make people feel uncomfortable today. One of the most unacceptable points about it is the way the Christian characters treat Shylock. The whole plot treats him badly too – in the course of the action his servant leaves him to go and work for Bassanio, his daughter deceives him and deserts him to marry Lorenzo, taking large amounts of his cash with her. Then he loses his suit against Antonio and finds that, through his bond, he has committed a serious crime, the attempted murder of a Venetian citizen. His goods are forfeit, and though his life is spared he is obliged to renounce his religion and become a Christian. Was Shakespeare anti-semitic?

If he was, then he was no different from most of the rest of sixteenth-century society. Jews had been expelled from England in the reign of Edward III; although a few had remained in London they were obliged to profess Christianity. They were permitted to live in Venice, in a walled part of the city which was locked at night and which was known as the Ghetto . . .

Most people thought of Jews as if they were bogeymen. They were hated because they were said to have killed Christ, and were sometimes accused of killing and eating Christian children as part of their religious rites. On the stage they were presented as grotesque villains with big noses.

The whole mood of Elizabethan England was one of unthinking chauvinism. Nationalist propaganda was widespread.

Oh blessed peace, oh happy Prince, oh fortunate people. The living God is only the English God.

(John Lyly, 1580)

What country in Europe comparable to England? What more wonderful than London?

(Thomas Johnson, 1596)

The English . . . are powerful in the field, successful against their enemies . . . If they see a foreigner very well made or particularly handsome they will say 'It is a pity he is not an Englishman.'

(Paul Hentzner, 1598)

There was a steady stream of immigration into England, and particularly into London, from France, the Netherlands and from Ireland. In the 1590s a series of anti-alien riots broke out in London.

Two of the things that may have prompted Shakespeare to write a play with a Jew as a main character were (a) the Lopez case of 1594, and (b) a play by Marlowe, *The Jew of Malta*, which was a successful part of the repertoire of a rival theatre company.

(a) *The Lopez case*

Dr Roderigo Lopez was a Christianized Portuguese Jew who was appointed physician to the Queen in 1586. In 1594 he was accused by the Earl of Essex of plotting to poison the Queen. This was a dubious charge, and Elizabeth herself tried to intercede for Lopez. But in June he was hanged, drawn and quartered at Tyburn. Before his execution he is said to have shouted, 'I am a Christian and I love the Queen.' The crowd replied, 'Hang him, for he is a Jew.'

(b) *'The Jew of Malta'*

Marlowe was the only dramatist writing at the beginning of Shakespeare's career who presented him with any serious competition, and Marlowe's theatre company, the Lord Admiral's Men, rivalled Shakespeare's. In 1589 Marlowe's company had performed a play by him called *The Jew of Malta*. The plot deals with the wicked deeds of a Jew, a villainous miser called Barabas, whose daughter Abigail eventually turns against her father and becomes a Christian. In 1594 *The Jew of Malta* was revived for several performances at the time of the Lopez affair, and it remained a fairly popular piece. Shakespeare may have been interested in writing a play which would deal, much more subtly than Marlowe's blood and thunder story, with Jews in society.

The Venetian Ghetto

Mary McCarthy outlines the historical facts behind Venice's tradition of religious tolerance, and describes the city's treatment of its Jewish population in the sixteenth, seventeenth and eighteenth centuries:

The Venetians invented the income tax, statistical science, the floating of government stock, state censorship of books, anonymous denunciations (the Bocca del Leone), the gambling casino, and the Ghetto ... a typical piece of Venetian machinery, designed to 'contain' the Jews while profiting from them. The word comes from the Venetian word, foundry . . . The area of the New Foundry was an island, on which the Jews were shut up every day at nightfall. The three gates were closed and locked; Christian guards, paid by the Jews, were posted, at first in boats on the canal. The house windows facing outwards were blocked up, by decree, so that the Ghetto turned a blind face to the city . . .

The Venetians, needless to say, were alert to the picturesque aspect. The Ghetto became a tourist haunt almost as soon as it was devised. Thomas Coryat, an Englishman who walked from Somerset to Venice, described his peregrinations through the Ghetto in 1608. The Jews of that time were prosperous and handsome, the women, he said, 'as beautiful as I ever saw . . . so gorgeous in their apparel, jewels, chains of gold, and rings adorned with precious stones' . . .

The Venetian Jews, in their red hats, were called on to supply learning, lore, and luxurious appointments for the foreign world. Henry VIII enlisted the opinion of a Venetian rabbi in his divorce suit against Katherine of Aragon . . .

The authorities would not permit the Jews to be persecuted . . . the right to do arbitrary violence to Jewish persons and property – a right that appeared virtually innate to the rest of the Christian world. That, on the contrary, a Jew had rights, was the essence of Venetian law, whose spirit is summed up, correctly, by Shakespeare's merchant, Antonio:

> The Duke cannot deny the course of law,
> For the commodity that strangers have
> With us in Venice, if it be denied,
> Will much impeach the justice of the state,
> Since that the trade and profit of the city
> Consisteth of all nations.

> (III. 3. 26–31)

'The trade and profit of the city' – here the Venetian cash-register rings, for if the Republic tolerated the Jews, it did so for a price. No Jew, including a native, could stay in Venice without a permit, which cost a considerable sum of money . . . The notion that a Jew had rights did not imply any doctrine of equality; the Jews had *specific* rights, the rights he paid to enjoy.

The Venetians exacted a veritable pound of flesh. They bled the Jewish community in every conceivable way. Since the law forbade Jews to own land, the Republic forced them to *rent* the Ghetto in its entirety on a long lease; the day the Jews moved in, rentals were raised one-third. In the course of years, many Jews left Venice for Holland, because of Venetian rapacity; others died of the plague. But the community continued to pay rent on houses that stood unoccupied – that was the contract. They were gouged for taxes, for tribute, for the army, for the navy, for the upkeep of the canals; they were forced to keep open their loan banks and to pay the government for the privilege, long after these had ceased to be profitable. They were not permitted to go out of business. This relentless policy continued to the point where, in 1735, the *Inquisitori sopra gli Ebrei* had to confess to the Senate that the Jews under their supervision were insolvent, and the community was declared bankrupt, by official state decree. There was no more to be got from them, the Venetians, as realists, conceded, crossing the account off their books with one of these resigned shrugs commonly thought of as Jewish . . .

The Jews were the last representatives of the Eastern bazaars to remain in Venice; when the Star of David set in the eighteenth-century Ghetto, Venice herself was extinguished.

(Mary McCarthy, *Venice Observed*, Heinemann, 1961)

Venice and Belmont

Venice and Belmont are very different places. Belmont is a kind of earthly paradise; Venice is a worldly city, dedicated to commerce and competition. W. H. Auden reflects on the differences – and the similarities:

Without the Venice scenes, Belmont would be an Arcadia without any relation to actual times and places, and where, therefore, money and sexual love have no reality of their own, but are symbolic signs for a community in a state of grace. But Belmont is related to Venice though their existences are not really compatible with each other. This incompatibility is brought out in a fascinating way by the difference between Belmont time and Venice time. Though we are not told exactly how long the period is before Shylock's loan must be repaid, we know that it is more than a month. Yet Bassanio goes off to Belmont immediately, submits immediately on arrival to the test of the caskets, and has just triumphantly passed it when Antonio's letter arrives to inform him that Shylock is about to take him to court and claim his pound of flesh. Belmont, in fact, is like one of those enchanted palaces where time stands still. But because we are made aware of Venice, the real city, where time is real, Belmont becomes a real society to be judged by the same standards we apply to any other kind of society. Because of Shylock and Antonio, Portia's inherited fortune becomes real money which must have been made in this world, as all fortunes are made, by toil, anxiety, the enduring and inflicting of suffering. Portia we can admire because, having seen her leave her Earthly Paradise to do a good deed in this world (one notices, incidentally, that in this world she appears in disguise), we know that she is aware of her wealth as a moral responsibility, but the other inhabitants of Belmont, Bassanio, Gratiano, Lorenzo and Jessica, for all their beauty and charm, appear as frivolous members of a leisure class, whose care-free life is parasitic upon the labours of others, including usurers.

(W. H. Auden, *The Dyer's Hand*, Faber & Faber, 1963)

Richard II

39, 40. *Richard Pasco and Ian Richardson, as Bolingbroke and Richard* II *in the mirror scene – in rehearsal and in performance.*

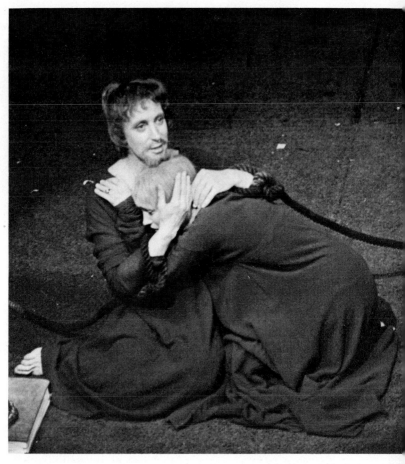

41. '*And must we be divided? Must we part?*' Richard and his queen, about to be taken to separate prisons. *Royal Shakespeare Company, 1973.*

42. '*Such is the breath of kings.*' *Richard and Bolingbroke, Royal Shakespeare Company, 1973.*

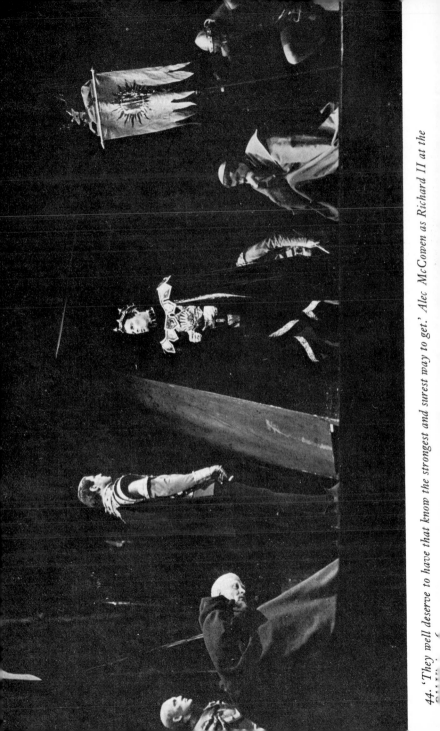

44. 'They well deserve to have that know the strongest and surest way to get.' Alec McCowen as Richard II at the

(in order of appearance)

Michael Aspel	*presenter*
Toby Robertson	*director*
Ian McKellen	*actor*
Harry Dalton	*teacher*
Donald Sinden	*actor*
Timothy West	*actor*

MICHAEL ASPEL:

We're back to the fourteenth century with *Richard II*, one of our Shakespeare history plays. The official meaning of the word 'history' is 'a record of past events, their cause and importance'. Can the men who made history tell us what it is? Napoleon said, 'History is but a fable agreed upon.' And guess who said, 'Anybody can make history; only a great man can write it.' Oscar Wilde of course, and to his fellow playwrights history has been a fertile area for pageantry and philosophy. You shouldn't be knocked out by surprise to learn that Shakespeare, who wrote his History plays about medieval kings dead long before his own days, had some very modern ideas to apply.

Cast your imagination back to 29th April 1398. Richard II's court was a lavish affair. He was surrounded by sycophants who were grovelling to his kingly power and it is this power that attracted Shakespeare's imagination. His documentation of Richard II is best thought of, not simply as a History play, but as a mirror reflecting the dilemmas and the struggles within his own Elizabethan society. The play is first and foremost political. Toby Robertson, who has directed a celebrated *Richard II*, dislikes the tendency to dismiss Shakespeare's History plays as mere period pieces with fine patches of poetry. It's just too easy to label them 'History' and put them back into a dusty corner. In fact, there's often, as we've noted, quite a lot of contemporary relevance.

TOBY ROBERTSON:

We are looking at very tough plays about a society in disintegration, which is exactly what the Elizabethan period was. There is most power at the extremities, the polarities are strong. This is very much what was happening in the Elizabethan and Jacobean times. And I would think that this is the sort of approach to take to a play like *Richard II*. It has been seen as rather a beautiful, exquisite, narcissistic piece, but I don't think that's the way it ought to be approached.

MICHAEL ASPEL:

It's easy to see why *Richard II* has been taken for a narcissistic play. Richard himself is a great scene stealer, who makes superb speeches that punctuate his fall from power. Ian KcKellen was a memorable Richard. How did he approach the role of a man notorious for kingly incompetence?

IAN MCKELLEN:

Well, I won't cloud the issue by suggesting that, of course, Shakespeare is not actually writing about a real King Richard II at all. Shakespeare doesn't write history books; he writes plays which happen, in some cases, to be set in the past. But the character on the stage is a man in a predicament. And the predicament is that he believes himself to be not just a king, governing a cabinet, governing his nobles, governing a city, governing a country; more that Richard II thought himself to be a god, to have a direct link to the almighty.

MICHAEL ASPEL:

That's no poetic licence on Shakespeare's part. This idea was central to the way people in the medieval and Elizabethan world looked at their society.

HARRY DALTON:

I suppose anybody coming to *Richard II* for the first time is puzzled by the attitude to the King that all the people in the play show. Certainly the first time I ever saw *Richard II* I think it puzzled me. It wasn't until after I'd been to my first production of *Richard* that I remembered a hymn I used to sing at my junior school assembly, 'All things bright and beautiful'. One of the verses went: 'The rich man in his castle, the poor man at his gate. He made them high or lowly, and ordered their estate.' You don't hear this verse sung very much nowadays, perhaps because it illustrates an attitude that is no longer popular in our democratic days. But it shows that even a hundred years ago when this hymn was written an idea persisted that was much stronger in Shakespeare's day. The idea was that everything and every person in the universe had a place that was part of God's grand design. In short, the Elizabethans believed in what scholars call 'the great chain of being'. Everybody had a place; it wasn't just a place, it was really a rank. Shakespeare called it degree. The attitude to your place in the rank was something of tremendous importance. You can't really understand what is happening in the play unless you fully appreciate how the Elizabethans and people before them thought about the idea of the King. Incidentally it didn't matter very much whether the King was good or bad. That was God's business. The King was God's anointed deputy on earth and you had to accept the sort of king you had, and if it was a tyrant you had, then that was your hard luck.

MICHAEL ASPEL:

And it was hard luck to be one of Richard's subjects. In the early scenes of the play, there are suggestions that Richard is haughty and weak, perhaps even corrupt. It opens with his feeble and indecisive attempts to arbitrate between two unruly nobles, Bolingbroke and Mowbray. He orders them to settle their dispute in a tournament, but then he banishes them instead. He's very unpopular with his barons, grabbing money at the slightest excuse. And his corruption touches his own family. He is, to some extent, involved with the murder of his own uncle, the Duke of Gloucester. Yet this is the king who was 'not born to sue but to command'. Shakespeare was fascinated by Richard's sense of divine right, coupled with divine irresponsibility. Richard might well seem a difficult character to comprehend today.

IAN MCKELLEN:

When I was a boy, I read in the newspaper of a fairytale man in the north of India. There, there was a king, who was an emperor and who thought himself to be a god, who was worshipped by the Tibetans. He was the Dalai Lama, the highest sort of lama, the highest sort of holy man, that could be conceived. When his country was invaded by the Chinese, old neighbours, the Dalai Lama fled south further into India, where he's still alive today. He was a young man at the time. And he lost his kingdom and he stopped being a god. I don't know what the Dalai Lama feels like today but I think he went through the same predicament as Richard II. Knowing that there had been a man in almost the same position as Richard II made me feel, 'Well, perhaps I can understand him as much as I can understand the Dalai Lama.' During the course of the play when his cousin, Bolingbroke, gradually, insidiously takes over the running of the country, and Richard is deposed by force of arms and eventually divests himself of all the trappings of royalty – the crown, the sceptre – he declines from that state of divinity, and becomes a man.

MICHAEL ASPEL:

It's what a play should be – a chance to see people change. It's a cunning piece of writing, beautifully controlled, and you should note the passage where Shakespeare suggests change. Exam questions have asked: 'To what extent is Richard's story a tragedy?' or 'How does Shakespeare gain our sympathies for Richard?' Often the answer lies in a particular speech. Perhaps one of the most potent for setting the scene for a tragedy is the long speech that Bolingbroke's father, John of Gaunt, makes to his brother, the Duke of York. These two old uncles of Richard are torn between duty to king and to country.

DONALD SINDEN:

> Methinks I am a prophet new-inspired,
> And thus, expiring, do foretell of him:
> His rash fierce blaze of riot cannot last;
> For violent fires soon burn out themselves.
> Small showers last long, but sudden storms are short.
> He tires betimes that spurs too fast betimes.
> With eager feeding food doth choke the feeder.
> Light vanity, insatiate cormorant,
> Consuming means, soon preys upon itself.
> This royal throne of kings, this sceptred isle,
> This earth of majesty, this seat of Mars,
> This other Eden – demi-paradise –
> This fortress built by nature for herself
> Against infection and the hand of war,
> This happy breed of men, this little world,
> This precious stone set in the silver sea,
> Which serves it in the office of a wall,
> Or as a moat defensive to a house
> Against the envy of less happier lands;
> This blessèd plot, this earth, this realm, this England,
> This nurse, this teeming womb of royal kings,
> Feared by their breed, and famous by their birth,
> Renownèd for their deeds as far from home
> For Christian service and true chivalry
> As is the sepulchre in stubborn Jewry
> Of the world's ransom, blessèd Mary's son;
> This land of such dear souls, this dear dear land,
> Dear for her reputation through the world,
> Is now leased out – I die pronouncing it –
> Like to a tenement or pelting farm.
> England, bound in with the triumphant sea,
> Whose rocky shore beats back the envious siege
> Of watery Neptune, is now bound in with shame,
> With inky blots and rotten parchment bonds.
> That England that was wont to conquer others
> Hath made a shameful conquest of itself.
> Ah, would the scandal vanish with my life,
> How happy then were my ensuing death!

(II. 1. 31–68)

MICHAEL ASPEL:

On his very death-bed, Gaunt challenges Richard, and Richard hastily calls his uncle 'a lean-witted fool'. And, on an embittered family note, Gaunt dies, while Richard takes all the money that was his cousin Bolingbroke's. At an early stage of the play, Shakespeare signposts Richard's spontaneous and foolish actions. Gaunt warned him of the 'thousand flatterers' that 'sit within thy crown', but Richard marches arrogantly on. His other uncle, the Duke of York, says that if he takes from Bolingbroke what by law is his, Richard will 'take from Time/His charters and his customary rights'. But Richard, subsidized by Bolingbroke's inheritance, goes to war in Ireland, leaving York as his regent, and leaving the way open for his exiled cousin to return to England with the excuse of claiming his title and money. Shakespeare introduces the warmer side of Richard's nature here – oh yes, he has one. For the first time we see that Richard is loved as well as hated. His friends, Bushy, Bagot and Green, comfort his young queen, Isabel. But Bolingbroke appears with the quiet resolution of a man who knows exactly what he must do, and he disposes of Bushy and Green. The scene is set for the struggle of the two cousins. It's the first chance that we have to get our teeth into the character of Bolingbroke. What did Timothy West note about the role at this point?

TIMOTHY WEST:

Bolingbroke has got everybody behind him, he's a handsome man, a wronged man, and he has birth and connections. Of course, historically, he was an extremely cultivated and very popular man, and he was businesslike.

MICHAEL ASPEL:

Ah, but beneath this lurks a sinister character. There isn't anything sinister about this exam question on Bolingbroke.

TIMOTHY WEST:

'Shakespeare certainly shows us the efficiency and shrewdness of Bolingbroke as a politician but he also shows us his hypocrisy and ruthlessness. What evidence do you find in the play for these characteristics of Bolingbroke?' Well, simply through reading all the scenes in which Bolingbroke appears.

> BOLINGBROKE
> Bushy and Green, I will not vex your souls,
> Since presently your souls must part your bodies,
> With too much urging your pernicious lives,
> For 'twere no charity. Yet, to wash your blood
> From off my hands, here in the view of men
> I will unfold some causes of your deaths.
> You have misled a prince, a royal king,
> A happy gentleman in blood and lineaments,
> By you unhappied and disfigured clean.
> You have in manner with your sinful hours
> Made a divorce betwixt his Queen and him,
> Broke the possession of a royal bed,
> And stained the beauty of a fair queen's cheeks
> With tears drawn from her eyes by your foul wrongs.
> Myself – a prince by fortune of my birth,
> Near to the King in blood, and near in love,
> Till you did make him misinterpret me –
> Have stooped my neck under your injuries,
> And sighed my English breath in foreign clouds,
> Eating the bitter bread of banishment . . .
>
> (III. 1. 2–21)

There is evidence, I think, in that speech that he argues his own cause through apparently arguing Richard's cause and the Queen's cause. He's very, very careful to keep in with all the electorate as much as possible at this stage. That, I suppose, is a kind of hypocrisy but it seems to me that, in his position, it's an arguable political move.

MICHAEL ASPEL:

His behaviour certainly throws old York into a spin because he really doesn't know where his allegiance lies. He says despairingly that both are his kinsmen. One, a divinely appointed King – the other, his kinsman whom the King has wronged.

IAN McKELLEN:

Richard and Bolingbroke were presumably brought up as kids together. They went their separate ways in manhood. But it was a great shock to Richard to feel that his cousin, someone in his family, should knock him off the throne. *Richard II* is a family play. Aumerle, the Duke of York's son, is another cousin. You could say the play is about three cousins – Richard, Bolingbroke and Aumerle.

MICHAEL ASPEL:

Aumerle is loyal to Richard on his return from Ireland and together they face political upheavals.

IAN McKELLEN:

The politics of *Richard II* are being repeated almost daily in our lives today. At the time I was playing Richard II in 1968 and 1969, Czechoslovakia, a communist country, was being run by a politician called Dubček. He was leading his country away from the East and towards the West and, for his pains, he was overrun by the Russian tanks in a famous invasion. Dubček was imprisoned and tortured and, although he is alive today, he's not alive to tell the tale because he's in some very lowly job in Czechoslovakia; the old previous order which he had tried to change overruled him. The amazing parallel between that situation and the play of *Richard II* is that the Russians have always been close neighbours of the Czechs and the Slovaks, and they have always been looked on as allies. They are in a sense the equivalent to Richard II's cousin Bolingbroke. And when the Russians, the cousins of the Czechs and the Slovaks, invaded, the impact on the Czechs and the Slovaks was horrific. I know that because I played Richard II in Czechoslovakia six months after Dubček had fallen and the Russians had arrived and taken over the country. I came to the speech, which is Richard's return from Ireland, where he's been putting down the rebellion there. He comes back and, aware of his inferior forces compared with Bolingbroke's increasing power, he kneels down on the ground and asks the earth to help him. That's what the Czechs and

Slovaks had done when the Russian tanks had come into their country and Dubček was going to fall. They too knew that they had nothing but themselves and the ground. And when I did this speech in Bratislava, which is a capital town in Czechoslovakia, I could hear the audience crying, crying! – at a speech by a playwright of a foreign country, Shakespeare, who had lived all those years ago but who understood the dilemma that they had just lived through, six months before.

> Needs must I like it well. I weep for joy
> To stand upon my kingdom once again.
> Dear earth, I do salute thee with my hand,
> Though rebels wound thee with their horses' hoofs.
> As a long-parted mother with her child
> Plays fondly with her tears and smiles in meeting,
> So weeping, smiling, greet I thee, my earth,
> And do thee favours with my royal hands.
> Feed not thy sovereign's foe, my gentle earth,
> Nor with thy sweets comfort his ravenous sense,
> But let thy spiders that suck up thy venom
> And heavy-gaited toads, lie in their way,
> Doing annoyance to the treacherous feet
> Which with usurping steps do trample thee.
> Yield stinging nettles to mine enemies;
> And when they from thy bosom pluck a flower
> Guard it, I pray thee, with a lurking adder,
> Whose double tongue may with a mortal touch
> Throw death upon thy sovereign's enemies.
> Mock not my senseless conjuration, lords.
> This earth shall have a feeling, and these stones
> Prove armèd soldiers ere her native king
> Shall falter under foul rebellion's arms.
>
> (III. 2. 4–26)

HARRY DALTON:

Perhaps the whole process of the play can be described as the gradual impinging of reality upon the fantasy world that Richard has built around himself and, indeed, inside himself.

> Let's talk of graves, of worms, and epitaphs;
> Make dust our paper, and with rainy eyes

> Write sorrow on the bosom of the earth.
> Let's choose executors and talk of wills –
> And yet not so; for what can we bequeath
> Save our deposed bodies to the ground?
> Our lands, our lives, and all are Bolingbroke's,
> And nothing can we call our own but death
> And that small model of the barren earth
> Which serves as paste and cover to our bones.
> For God's sake let us sit upon the ground
> And tell sad stories of the death of kings –
>
> (III. 2. 145–56)

When confronted by adversity, he doesn't meet it with strength. He doesn't always meet it with dignity. He's very given to self-chastisement, to self-pity: public expressions of self-pity which are, I think, and should be in the play, embarrassing to those who watch.

MICHAEL ASPEL:

Yes, a king who compares his crown to a well 'That owes two buckets, filling one another,/The emptier ever dancing in the air,/The other down, unseen, and full of water', and concludes: 'That bucket down and full of tears am I', is full of self-pity. When Richard hands over his crown to Bolingbroke and foreswears all pomp and majesty, he has plenty of reason to feel sorry for himself. The agony is prolonged by the slow, inverted coronation in which the crown is last to go. Richard does retain one crown to the play's end. 'You may my glories and my state depose,/But not my griefs. Still am I king of those.' But we can't properly judge Richard's growth to manhood and understanding until he's alone, because if you give him an audience he puts on a show. Even in the brief scene of parting from his wife, he finds room to dramatize his misery. 'Tell thou the lamentable tale of me,/and send the hearers weeping to their beds.' It's in Pomfret Castle prison that we finally lament him.

TIMOTHY WEST:
                    Music do I hear.
Ha, ha, keep time. How sour sweet music is
When time is broke, and no proportion kept!
So is it in the music of men's lives;
And here have I the daintiness of ear
To check time broke in a disordered string,
But for the concord of my state and time,
Had not an ear to hear my true time broke.
I wasted time, and now doth time waste me;
For now hath time made me his numbering clock.
My thoughts are minutes, and with sighs they jar
Their watches on unto mine eyes, the outward watch
Whereto my finger, like a dial's point,
Is pointing still in cleansing them from tears.
Now, sir, the sound that tells what hour it is
Are clamorous groans which strike upon my heart,
Which is the bell. So sighs, and tears, and groans
Show minutes, times, and hours. But my time
Runs posting on in Bolingbroke's proud joy,
While I stand fooling here, his jack of the clock.
This music mads me. Let it sound no more;
For though it have holp madmen to their wits,
In me it seems it will make wise men mad.
Yet blessing on his heart that gives it me;
For 'tis a sign of love, and love to Richard
Is a strange brooch in this all-hating world.
                              (V. 5. 41–66)

MICHAEL ASPEL:

'Love to Richard.' That's been the theme since Scene One and
it's only moments before his murder that Richard recognizes his
self-indulgence and his own vanity. He's exposed to himself as
well as to his enemies. And none is more treacherous than Exton,
who takes the law into his own hands when he kills an anointed
king. Richard dies with extreme courage, and Exton recognizes
the disastrous nature of this deed too late. 'As full of valour as of
royal blood./Both have I spilled.' The throne is now Boling-

broke's by death as well as deposition, and it's a dangerous inheritance.

TIMOTHY WEST:

If you're playing Bolingbroke, you often have a problem, I think, with the very last scene. The question that you've got to ask yourself is: 'How much of a shock is it when you're confronted by Richard's body?' I don't think it's a factual shock, but I do think it's a huge emotional shock to him because this is the moment, really the first moment in the play, when he becomes aware of the appalling responsibilities of kingship which stay with him and begin to destroy him as a man all through *Henry IV, Part 1*. It's interesting that the imagery of growth, of harvest, that has been used so much through the play, is used in this last speech when he says: 'Lords, I protest, my soul is full of woe/That blood should sprinkle me to make me grow.' It's a terrible prophecy. It's a reign which is entirely fed by blood.

MICHAEL ASPEL:

In *Henry IV, Part 1*, Shakespeare explores Bolingbroke's growth in the world of politics. In *Richard II*, he gives us the disintegration of a king, the collapse of an ego. In both plays history is the dramatization of the past but, as Timothy West and Ian McKellen acknowledge, Shakespeare wrote not for an age, but for all time.

TIMOTHY WEST:

Richard II, of course, is a very different sort of play from *Henry IV, Part 1*, because you haven't got the big, central, comic character. It's much more a political play.

IAN MCKELLEN:

There is no political situation in the whole of Shakespeare, there is no emotional situation, there is no family situation, there is no joke – there is nothing which cannot be related to a specific parallel situation in our own experience of modern life.

The Tudor view of history

The Tudors, from Henry VII to Elizabeth I, were great public relations experts and manipulators of history. The period covered by Shakespeare's History plays – from Richard II to Richard III – was of paramount importance in their propaganda version of history. In this version, the deposition of King Richard II was a great wrong which resulted in a century of civil war and popular unrest. The accession of Henry VII, Henry Tudor, in 1485, marked the end of this period of unrest and the beginning of a new era of peaceful rule by divinely appointed kings. The Tudors were strong promoters of the doctrine of the divine right of kings, and the deposition of Richard II was therefore, in their book, a very heavy crime indeed. He had been king by the right of hereditary succession and also by the appointment of God.

At the same time, however, Richard II was famous for his extravagance, the corruption of his court, and the taxes and loans he wrung out of his subjects. His reliance on favourites and flatterers, rather than on the advice of experienced ministers, was notorious. His name was also habitually linked with the murder of his uncle, the Duke of Gloucester. Did Richard's criminal behaviour perhaps justify the crime of deposing him? Strict Tudor policy said not. In 1571 an official sermon, *Against Disobedience and Wilful Rebellion*, contained the following passage:

What shall we then do to an evil, to an unkind Prince, an enemy to us, hated of God, hurtful to the Commonwealth? Lay no violent hand upon him, saith good David, but let live until God appoint, and work his end, either by natural death, or in war by lawful enemies, not by traitorous subjects.

Elizabeth I was sometimes compared to Richard II in the political discussions of her time. Like him, she lacked an obvious heir. She was often accused of being ruled by favourites. Being continually short of money, she was given to inventing new forms of taxation, and to selling off royal monopolies.

However, her supporters and apologists consistently presented Elizabeth as the embodiment of peace and prosperity. Shakespeare was one of several Elizabethan playwrights writing history plays; it was a popular genre, and helped to promote the Tudor view of history. *The True Tragedie of Richard III*, a play by an unknown author which was printed in 1594, ended with a glowing speech of praise for Elizabeth:

> She is that lamp that keeps fair Englands light,
> And through her faith her country lives in peace:
> And she hath put proud Antichrist to flight,
> And been the means that civil wars did cease.
> Then England kneel upon thy hairy knee,
> And thank that God that still provides for thee.

'I am Richard the Second, know ye not that?'

In 1601 the Earl of Essex, who had been one of Queen Elizabeth's favourites, was under a cloud. In the previous year he had been arrested because he was suspected of ambitions towards the crown. Though he was released, it seemed very unlikely that he would ever regain his former position and enjoy the Queen's trust again. In February 1601, a group of his friends joined him in plotting an outright rebellion against the Queen and her ministers. Some of the lords who were involved went to the Globe Theatre and arranged for Shakespeare's *Richard II* to be put on by Shakespeare's company on 7 February – the day before the coup that they were planning. Despite the company's protest that the play was 'old and out of use' and would not attract much of an audience, the performance took place. The next day Essex led his abortive rebellion, charging up Fleet Street into the City, but finding no support among the citizens whom he had hoped to mobilize. He was sent to the Tower and, three weeks later, executed.

There is good evidence that Queen Elizabeth very much disliked the play and thought that it was politically dangerous. During her lifetime one scene – Act IV, Scene 1, the deposition scene – was cut out of the printed version of the play, and was probably not allowed to be performed in the theatre either. The political climate towards the end of Elizabeth's reign was far too touchy for it to be safe to show the deposition of a king on the public stage.

Queen Elizabeth herself, in a recorded conversation with an official historian, once remarked: 'I am Richard the Second. Know ye not that?' and bitterly added, of the Earl of Essex, 'He that will forget God, will also forget his benefactors; this tragedy was played forty times in open streets and houses.'

The divine right of kings

It was part of the conventional philosophy of Shakespeare's time that the health of any country depended on the nature of its ruler. This belief was stated strongly in the preface of an Elizabethan classic, *A Mirror for Magistrates*:

The goodness or badness of any realm lieth in the goodness or badness of the rulers. And therefore not without great cause do the holy Apostles so earnestly charge us to pray for the magistrates; for indeed the wealth and quiet of every common weal, the disorder also and miseries of the same, come specially through them.

However, even if the king was a bad or weak king, this was not felt to justify anyone in deposing him or rebelling against him. For kings were thought to be appointed by God. It was for God alone, therefore, to overthrow a bad ruler:

Whosoever rebelleth against any ruler either good or bad rebelleth against God and shall be sure of a wretched end, for God cannot but maintain his deputy.

But one of the reasons why Shakespeare is such an interesting writer is that he never presents a one-sided case. Though he must have been thoroughly used to the idea of divine right, in *Richard II* he did not write a play which was simply about the wickedness of deposing God's anointed king. He showed some of Richard's bad habits, his callousness, his extravagance, and his weakness. Then, especially in the second half of the play, he stressed the strength of Richard's belief in his own position, showed him as every inch a king, and emphasized what was likely to happen if Bolingbroke persisted in his attempt to seize the throne. Bolingbroke is shown as a much more politically convincing figure than Richard. He is strong, efficient, popular and reserved – but he is a usurper.

Other sixteenth-century writers had wrestled with the question of whether a weak king was better than a strong ruler without any legitimate title to the throne. In 1528 William Tyndale wrote:

Yea, and it is better to have a tyrant unto thy king: than a shadow; a passive king that doth nought himself, but suffereth others to do with him what they will, and to lead him whither they list. For a tyrant, though he do wrong unto the good, yet he punisheth the evil, and maketh all men obey . . . A king that is as soft as silk and effeminate . . . shall be much more grievous unto the realm than a right tyrant.

The prophecies in *Richard II*

Because *Richard II* is the first in a cycle of plays which show the events that followed the deposition of Richard, it is a play that looks forward a good deal. A lot is said at various points in the play about the possible consequence of present actions. Both of Richard's uncles, Gaunt and York, point out what his rash behaviour may lead to. Gaunt warns him of the danger of being led by flatterers, and dwells on the shame of his habit of selling royal tax rights for ready cash. When, after Gaunt's death, Richard announces his decision to seize his dead uncle's goods and property, all of which belongs by rights to Gaunt's son Bolingbroke, the Duke of Hereford, York's outraged outburst is truly prophetic:

> Take Hereford's rights away, and take from Time
> His charters and his customary rights.
> Let not tomorrow then ensue today.

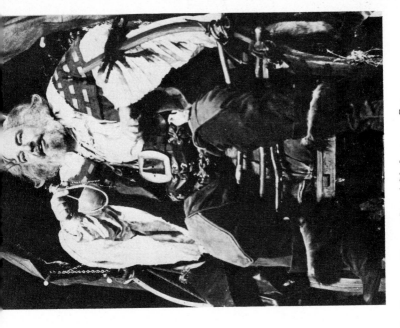

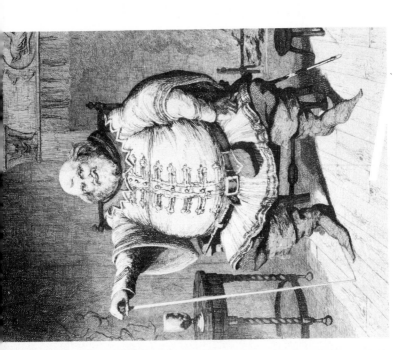

45, 46. *Falstaff, drawn by George Cruikshank (1857) and played by Brewster Mason (Royal Shakespeare Company, 1975).*

47. *The Boar's Head Tavern. Two scenes from the Prospect Theatre Company's 1974 production.*

48. *Falstaff plays the King.*

9. *The death of Hotspur. Alan Howard as Prince Hal. Royal Shakespeare*
Company, 1975.

50. A scene from Orson Welles's film version of the Henry IV plays, Chimes at Midnight.

> Be not thyself; for how art thou a king
> But by fair sequence and succession?
>
> (II. 1. 195–9)

But the direst prophecies in the play concern the deposing of Richard. In a long speech, the Bishop of Carlisle predicts the chaos that will follow if Bolingbroke seizes the crown:

> The blood of English shall manure the ground,
> And future ages groan for this foul act.
> Peace shall go sleep with Turks and infidels,
> And in this seat of peace tumultuous wars
> Shall kin with kin, and kind with kind, confound.
> Disorder, horror, fear, and mutiny
> Shall here inhabit, and this land be called
> The field of Golgotha and dead men's skulls.
>
> (IV. 1. 137–44)

This speech looks forward to the events of *Henry IV, Parts 1* and *2*, and to the Wars of the Roses.

Richard himself speaks one of the most powerfully prophetic speeches in the play to the treacherous Northumberland, who has been Bolingbroke's chief agent in engineering his downfall:

> Northumberland, thou ladder wherewithal
> The mounting Bolingbroke ascends my throne,
> The time shall not be many hours of age
> More than it is ere foul sin, gathering head,
> Shall break into corruption. Thou shalt think,
> Though he divide the realm and give thee half,
> It is too little, helping him to all . . .
>
> (V. 1. 55–61)

This memorable prophecy is recalled by Bolingbroke when he is king, in *Henry IV, Part 2*. Shakespeare, deliberately quoting his own earlier play, underlines the force of the prophecy by making King Henry repeat King Richard's very words:

> But which of you was by –
> . . . When Richard, with his eye brimful of tears,
> Then checked and rated by Northumberland,

> Did speak these words, now proved a prophecy?
> 'Northumberland, thou ladder by the which
> My cousin Bolingbroke ascends my throne' –
> Though then, God knows, I had no such intent
> But that necessity so bowed the state
> That I and greatness were compelled to kiss –
> 'The time shall come' – thus did he follow it –
> 'The time will come that foul sin, gathering head,
> Shall break into corruption' – so went on,
> Foretelling this same time's condition,
> And the division of our amity.
>
> (*Henry IV, Part 2*, III. 1. 61–75)

It seems clear that Shakespeare's intention here was to stress the relationship between the plays in his cycle, and to point out how accurate the many prophetic statements in *Richard II* actually proved.

The staircase of history

In the following passage Jan Kott, writing about Shakespeare's History plays, is using the image of a grand staircase as a metaphor for history.

It was on a staircase that Leopold Jessner set *Richard III* in his famous production. . . The metaphor has philosophical consequences and is also dramatically fruitful. There are no good and bad kings; there are only kings on different steps of the same stairs. The names of the kings may change, but it is always a Henry who pushes a Richard down, or the other way round. Shakespeare's Histories are *dramatis personae* of the Grand Mechanism. But what is this Grand Mechanism which starts operating at the foot of the throne and to which the whole kingdom is subjected? A mechanism whose cog-wheels are both great lords and hired assassins; a mechanism which forces people to violence, cruelty and treason; which constantly claims new victims? A mechanism according to whose laws the road to power is at the same time the way to death? This Grand Mechanism is for Shakespeare the order of history, in which the king is the Lord's Anointed.

> Not all the water in the rough rude sea
> Can wash the balm off from an anointed king;
> The breath of worldly men cannot depose
> The deputy elected by the Lord.

(III. 2. 54–7)

The sun circles round the earth, and with it the spheres, planets and stars, all arranged in a hierarchic order. There is in the universe an order of the elements, an order of angelic choirs, and a corresponding order of rank on earth. There are superiors and vassals of the vassals. Royal power comes from God, and all power on earth is merely a reflection of the power wielded by the King.

Richard II is a tragedy of dethronement. It is, however, not just Richard's dethronement, but that of the King. Dethronement, in fact, of the idea of regal power . . . In *Richard II*, the Lord's Anointed, the King deprived of his crown, becomes a mere mortal. In the first acts of the tragedy the King was compared to the sun: others had to lower their eyes when faced with his dazzling Majesty. Now the sun has been hurled down from its orbit, and with it the entire order of the universe.

> . . . what can we bequeath
> Save our deposèd bodies to the ground?
> Our lands, our lives, and all are Bolingbroke's,
> And nothing can we call our own but death
> And that small model of the barren earth
> Which serves as paste and cover to our bones.
> . . .
> Throw away respect,
> Tradition, form, and ceremonious duty;
> For you have but mistook me all this while.
> I live with bread like you; feel want,
> Taste grief, need friends. Subjected thus,
> How can you say to me I am a king?

(III. 2. 149–54; 172–7)

There is no heaven and hell, no order of the spheres. The earth moves round the sun, and the history of the Renaissance is just a grand staircase, from the top of which ever-new kings fall into the abyss. There exists only the Grand Mechanism, but it is itself just a cruel and tragic farce.

Richard II is a tragedy of knowledge gained through experience. Just before being hurled into the abyss, the deposed King reaches the greatness of Lear. Slowly, step by step, King Lear walks down the grand staircase, to learn the whole cruelty of the world over which he had once ruled but which he did not know, and to drain the bitter cup to the dregs. Richard II is brutally and suddenly pushed into the abyss. But with him will founder the structure of the feudal world.

(Jan Kott, *Shakespeare Our Contemporary*, Methuen, 1964)

Henry IV, Part I

(in order of appearance)

Michael Aspel	*presenter*
John Barton	*director*
Sheridan Morley	*critic*
John Cox	*teacher*
Janet Suzman	*actress*
Patrick Stewart	*actor*
Timothy West	*actor*

MICHAEL ASPEL:

The last section dealt with the tragic tale of Richard II who lost both crown and life to the power-seeking Bolingbroke. This is the man whose fortunes we follow now, because he became King Henry IV.

When Henry usurped the throne, what he did effectively was give all dissatisfied noblemen an invitation to try to copy him, which they did. At the start of the play, Glendower is causing trouble in Wales, and we can see that the proud, impatient, young Harry Percy, known as Hotspur, will join the rebel cause given the merest chance. Henry IV's reign was one of public disruption and private sadness because his son and heir, Prince Hal, spent his day down at Mistress Quickly's pub with Peto and Poins, Bardolph and Falstaff. Falstaff, for all his charm, is a liar and a cheat. He wants to take the heir to the English throne on an excursion to Gad's Hill for a spot of robbery. All the same, Falstaff's lack of honour is just as exaggerated as Hotspur's honour. It's a play of contrasts, a quality John Barton admires. He chose this play to celebrate the bard's 400th birthday.

JOHN BARTON:

The *Henry IV* plays have always been among my very favourite plays of Shakespeare and I suppose one of the reasons is that they're rich and diverse in their texture: they're political, comic, tragic and pastoral in a way. The world goes from court to tavern to country to battlefield and back again, scene by scene. That richness and diversity has always pleased me.

PUPIL:

I'm studying the play and I think it's interesting to compare political dealings in the play with modern political dealings.

SHERIDAN MORLEY:

Henry IV was a pageant and a chronicle about power. It's not difficult to see Henry IV as the Nixon figure, the old man tired, worried by his past crimes, uneasy about the crown, uneasy about his family, uneasy about how long he can keep power. It's a power game for our time and for all time.

MICHAEL ASPEL:

The King's banishment of Mortimer early in the play is rather like the sudden dismissals and resignations of our politicians. And these bring about power shifts. Harry Hotspur and his dad, Northumberland, go over to Mortimer's party. They want to put him on the throne and push this 'ingrate and cankered Bolingbroke' off it. Of course, Shakespeare gives his rebels their own characters and reasons.

JOHN COX:

Shakespeare presents us with an almost bewildering variety of different types of ambition. We have the obvious idealism of Hotspur, rather naïve, not very practical.

PUPIL:

When I read the play, I found that Hotspur was just a hot-headed clown, fooling around with honour, rushing horses up hills, killing Scotsmen, and all this sort of thing.

JOHN COX:

We've got the shrewd, grasping nature of Worcester and Glendower – no unification of England for them; they're going to divide the country up. The King is trying to keep the status quo.

We've got a great contrast between the public and the private lives of the politicians.

MICHAEL ASPEL:

The King, in private, is a worried father. The Prince, in private, is a cold and calculating young man. The ruthless Glendower turns out to be quite fond of his daughter, and Hotspur has a wife, Kate.

JANET SUZMAN:

In all the male-oriented History plays (which they are on the whole), it's people like Kate Percy and Mistress Quickly, at the extreme other end of the scale, who provide absolutely delightful scenes of feminine persuasion and warmth and domesticity. They give people backgrounds, and homes, and delights. In these very mighty plays about politics, kingship, honour and war they tend to soften and humanize.

MICHAEL ASPEL:

She's a great humanizer, is Kate. It's a pity really that we see so little of her. But we needn't be depressed. This is a play with Falstaff after all, and he's one of those outsized and outrageous characters. He wasn't even silenced by his death in a later Shakespeare play. His comic spirit lived on in a novel by Robert Nye and an opera by Verdi. Falstaff's a free spirit, one you can't constrict to notions of good or bad.

JOHN BARTON:

I think you reduce him if you use either of the words 'good' or 'bad' about him. He is full of life and energy and panache and fun and devilment, and he's a bastard but he's very lovable – all the contradictions are true about him. He cries out to be rejected by Hal at the end but one's sad about it when Hal does so. Yet it is necessary for Hal, if he's going to be a king, to deal with him. One has to take a complex view of Falstaff, like one does about any rich character.

PATRICK STEWART:

I once understudied Falstaff and I was very privileged to watch an actor rehearse that part and then play it for a long Stratford season, an actor who for me has explored that character more fully than anyone else, and that was Paul Rogers. What I learnt about Falstaff through watching him was that there is, beside that energetic, turbulent, wilful, humorous spirit in Falstaff, a man who is small, narrow, mean, grotesquely selfish and self-centred, wicked and cruel, and I thought that he developed those two strands in the character extraordinarily well. There were always reasons why he did things – why he would take so much stick from Hal and the others, because it benefited him; and why he would finally abandon everyone and everything in order to save himself. One often hears of Falstaff, or sees him, being a kind of Father Christmas figure – a benevolent, jolly character – and I think it's important to find those vicious and violent elements in the man because they help to set off what is so funny and enjoyable about him.

MICHAEL ASPEL:

You can see why Hal, future King though he was, found this many-sided rogue attractive.

TIMOTHY WEST:

It's a universal story, I think. That relationship we can find in scores of couples we know, whether they're married or just good friends or business associates or whatever. There is that kind of deal between them: one of them does the thinking and perhaps provides money and resources for the other one, who is simply entertaining, is nice to be with.

MICHAEL ASPEL:

Falstaff is not ignorant of the world of politics that he rejects, and the examiners, bless them, haven't missed this point. Let's see how John Cox would tackle this old favourite: 'Falstaff's wit is not merely amusing; it provides a criticism of the world of serious affairs.'

JOHN COX:

We know he's a tremendously shrewd commentator on the political action. One thinks of his splendid caustic aside about Worcester in the final act: 'Rebellion lay in his way and he found it.'

MICHAEL ASPEL:

But he found a rival who was his match. King Henry is a good politician, too good, perhaps.

PUPIL:

When I first read the play, I didn't like him that much. I thought he was too careful to be a likeable character.

JOHN BARTON:

The King is a very rich character and it's a wonderful part when you put the two *Henry IV* plays alongside *Richard II*. Then you see Bolingbroke, from the man who usurped the crown from Richard in *Richard II* to the man who suffers the rest of his life for it in the *Henry IV* plays.

SHERIDAN MORLEY:

I believe that *Henry IV* is perhaps the most intensely political of all Shakespeare's plays. It gives you, perhaps not his greatest poetry, but his greatest insights into the making of power, and how power corrupts, and how it can be used for good and for bad. It gives you the two faces of young power in Hal and Hotspur – Hotspur, the golden boy, the King that never was, the son that Henry IV would like to have had instead of Hal. Hal gives you the other side of the coin – the seedier, uneasy, slightly drunken young man who is going to become, don't forget, Henry V.

MICHAEL ASPEL:

Sheridan Morley has hit upon something that interests the examiners. Here's the next question on the paper: 'What indications are there in the play that Prince Hal will later become a strong and serious-minded King?'

SHERIDAN MORLEY:

That first classic speech of Hal's in the tavern when Falstaff has played his first great trick. Hal pauses and says, really to the audience, 'I know you all,' meaning I know what's going to happen, I know that one day I'm going to have to put on the crown and I'm going to have to reject Falstaff and the pub and Mistress Quickly and the whole jokey tavern scene. The next question is: 'What do Falstaff's low companions contribute to the play?' Well, they contribute all kinds of things. They give you insights into Falstaff, that this man has to have people around him. He's a lonely man; we're never really told where he came from, what his father was like, what kind of childhood he had – the pub is really all he has. The way he manipulates his tavern friends and uses them and has to be their leader gives us a great insight, I think, into Falstaff. It's only with Falstaff's companions that you get the common man – the man who is never going to be a sergeant or a colonel, who is never going to be a prince or a king as a leader, who is never going to command even a rebel army, but who is going to have to be one of the soldiers.

MICHAEL ASPEL:

It is time to think of war. Hotspur is at home preparing the rebellion, and his wife knows something is up.

JANET SUZMAN:

'For what offence,' she asks him, 'have I this fortnight been/A banished woman from my Harry's bed?' (I don't think she means that they haven't slept in the same bed. She means that he hasn't turned towards her, made love to her, and that she finds rather strange.) 'Tell me, sweet lord, what is it that takes from thee/Thy stomach, pleasure, and thy golden sleep?' You get a terrific feeling of affection between the two. You also get a rather riven feeling, that he doesn't want to tell her the truth, and that he wants to allay her worrying by teasing her.

MICHAEL ASPEL:

So, Hotspur goes to join Glendower, promising his Kate that she shall follow the next day. What follows in the text is another of those rapid changes of scene and tone – from poetry and passion to chatty pub talk. Hal is there, and he promises everyone a rare treat. Falstaff is going to come in soon and start lying his head off about his adventures on Gad's Hill. Falstaff has gone to do a robbery, you remember, thinking the Prince and Poins were with him. But these two disappeared. They reappeared in disguise and they attacked Falstaff. Falstaff bursts into the pub and delights two audiences, one off and one on stage, with his tale of heroism, describing how he had fought off an ever-increasing number of men in the attempt to keep his ill-gotten gains. It's a good scene.

PATRICK STEWART:

Falstaff's lying is very interesting. When he tells the famous lie that lasts half a scene about 'seeing off the rogues in buckram', it's important to realize that he doesn't expect Hal to believe him; he just expects Hal to enjoy the show. He is a stand-up comic and that is his function. In the second play, *Henry IV, Part 2*, he becomes a more tragic figure simply because he represents a part of youth that Hal has to throw off in order to become a king, which for Shakespeare meant becoming divine in an odd way. So Falstaff is part of the energy that has to be rejected. But in this play he represents the comic spirit in Shakespeare more exactly than any other character.

PUPIL:

When I was studying the play, the most enjoyable sequence was the Gad's Hill part, where all the other characters realize that Falstaff is lying about the robbery, and he brilliantly turns the tables, saying – after Poins has said, 'Come, let's hear, Jack,

what trick hast thou now?' 'By the Lord, I knew ye as well ...
I was now a coward on instinct.'

MICHAEL ASPEL:

Falstaff admits he's beaten with such charm and wit and vitality
that the others egg him on to the next outrage. This is a key
moment in the play. All around the forces of war are gathering.
The King sends a messenger down to his disreputable son to
attend an interview at court. And Falstaff decides to put Hal
through a dummy run.

PUPIL:

First Falstaff plays King Henry and then the Prince has enough
of this joke and takes over as the King, and Falstaff has to play
Hal.

PRINCE HAL ... Thou art violently carried away from grace. There
is a devil haunts thee in the likeness of an old fat man, a tun of man is
thy companion. Why dost thou converse with that trunk of humours,
that bolting-hutch of beastliness, that swollen parcel of dropsies,
that huge bombard of sack, that stuffed cloak-bag of guts, that
roasted Manningtree ox with the pudding in his belly, that reverend
Vice, that grey Iniquity, that Father Ruffian, that Vanity in years?
Wherein is he good, but to taste sack and drink it? Wherein neat and
cleanly, but to carve a capon and eat it? Wherein cunning, but in
craft? Wherein crafty, but in villainy? Wherein villainous, but in all
things? Wherein worthy, but in nothing?
FALSTAFF I would your grace would take me with you. Whom means
your grace?
PRINCE HAL That villainous abominable misleader of youth, Falstaff,
that old white-bearded Satan.

(II. 4. 435–50)

And you tend to think of Falstaff comparing him with the real
King, and to think 'Which is the better father?' I think you
always end up on the side of the King because Falstaff is a bit of a
rogue all the time.

MICHAEL ASPEL:

And that's why you know all along that one day Hal will reject Falstaff. We realize that Hal will go to his father the next day and join his cause. But in the meantime Shakespeare sends us down to Wales where the rebels are carving up the map and sound as if they'd be quite happy to carve one another up too. Hotspur is argumentative and ill-mannered to Glendower and, when they join the ladies, he's no more polite.

JANET SUZMAN:

He says, 'Come, Kate, thou art perfect in lying down.' Rather rude but rather nice. 'Come, quick, quick, that I may lay my head in thy lap.' Nice double meaning there which you can all work out for yourselves. And she says, 'Go, ye giddy goose.' She's obviously a bit embarrassed by that but she likes it. And Hotspur says, 'Now I perceive the devil understands Welsh.' This is probably all very *sotte voce* to each other while this lilting Welsh ballad is going on. 'Lie still, ye thief, and hear the lady sing in Welsh.' And he's very rude and says, 'I had rather hear Lady my brach [that means my hound] howl in Irish.' We don't see them together again, sadly enough. You've got to think of these two, his head in her lap, their teasing badinage going on underneath the Welsh song, and the war just about to come. And the next time we see Kate it's all happened.

JOHN COX:

By the time the King summons Hal to him in Act III, he is perhaps beginning to feel his age that little bit more. He is aware of his overall power, he is optimistic about the future as far as the rebels are concerned but he's very depressed about his son. I think this is very analogous in contemporary terms. A father, perhaps middle-aged, of a different generation, well aware he's sown his own wild oats, and made his mistakes, but not wanting his son to do the same.

MICHAEL ASPEL:

Now is Hal's chance to redeem himself and he takes it. But he doesn't give in entirely to his father, because Falstaff goes with him to the war, and Falstaff behaves atrociously. While all the princes and dukes around him are going on diplomatic missions, Falstaff is inevitably drinking, and discoursing on death and honour. He puts an ironic perspective on the rest of the proceedings, and his presence reminds us that Hal could not stay with him in the tavern. What is comic behaviour in Falstaff would be chaos for a whole country in its King. It's at this point you need to ask yourself whether Falstaff is to be condemned or humoured.

SHERIDAN MORLEY:

Falstaff is the other half of Hal. Falstaff is what Hal avoids being. Falstaff, on the other hand, is also the best of England. He is the yeoman stock.

TIMOTHY WEST:

Of course, we all sympathize with him. I mean, that famous honour speech – it makes total sense. I think it possibly makes more sense to modern audiences than it would have done to any but the most cynical of Shakespeare's audiences.

MICHAEL ASPEL:

The battle is on. The King has gained the support of his son but the rebels are losing more and more of their promised aid. When the King offers Worcester mercy, Worcester doesn't tell this to Hotspur, instead he forces his own weak army into the field.

SHERIDAN MORLEY:

Another question which you might be asked: 'Why do you think the rebellion failed?' Well, because in the end, the rebellion had to fail. The English had a love for the crown, even if it was a usurped crown, which it was in Henry IV's case. Even so he had now got the crown, he was King, and the English, I think, by this time had had enough rebellion; they'd had two hundred

years of rebellion. What they wanted now was a steady government, even if it meant staying with a rather corrupt monarchy.
And so the rebellion failed partly out of sheer exhaustion on the
part of the countrymen of England.

TIMOTHY WEST:

I read *Henry IV, Part 1* when I was at school, and it made such
an impression on me that I went straight on and read *Henry IV,
Part 2*, because I wanted to see what happened to everybody.
It's an extraordinary play in that it really has three heroes – Hal,
Falstaff and Hotspur – all of whom are to some extent working
against each other. It's extraordinary that Shakespeare had such
love and enthusiasm for them all, that they're all terribly attractive characters. And really in that Hal/Hotspur fight at the end
of the play one should feel that it could go either way and,
whichever way it goes, the one who dies is a tragic loss. It's
possibly, I think the best constructed of all Shakespeare's plays
and as such is enormously enjoyable to play.

The education of Prince Hal

Harold took me back to the midnight division and on the way said that he had been invited to dinner at the Palace to discuss Prince Charles's education ... He said it had gone on for a couple of hours because it was so interesting.
(Richard Crossman, *Diaries of a Cabinet Minister*, Hamish Hamilton, 1975)

So much of the action and the interest of both parts of *Henry IV* have to do with Prince Hal that the King himself is really not the dominant figure in this play about the events of his time. Though we are told in the opening lines of *Henry IV, Part 1* that only a year has passed since the King came to the throne, he already seems a tired man, harassed by the continual outbursts of war and rebellion that have marked his reign. He is a very different figure from the strong, efficient politician that he was shown to be as Bolingbroke in *Richard II*, and he appears much older.

Much of the plot of *Henry IV, Part 1* has to do with attempted rebellions against the King, but the theme of the play is the youth and education of the Prince who is to become Henry V. This becomes much clearer if *Henry IV, Parts 1* and *2* are read together. Both parts have roughly the same shape. In each, Prince Hal has to choose between two ways of life. In *Part 1* the choice, put simply, is between honour and chivalry on the one hand and sloth and cowardice on the other. In *Part 2* the focus shifts from military life to civil life, and the choice is between law and lawlessness.

In each play, also, the qualities that the Prince must choose between are brought to life on the stage and represented by characters in the play. Hotspur, in *Henry IV, Part 1*, stands for bravery and honour, indeed for an almost crazy obsession with it.

HOTSPUR
By heaven, methinks it were an easy leap

> To pluck bright honour from the pale-faced moon,
> Or dive into the bottom of the deep,
> Where fathom-line could never touch the ground,
> And pluck up drownèd honour by the locks,
> So he that doth redeem her thence might wear
> Without corrival all her dignities.

(I. 3. 199–205)

Falstaff is just the opposite, slothful, cynical about glory and war, and a coward 'on instinct'.

FALSTAFF ... Can honour set to a leg? No. Or an arm? No. Or take away the grief of a wound? No. Honour hath no skill in surgery then? No. What is honour? A word. What is in that word honour? What is that honour? Air. A trim reckoning! Who hath it? He that died a'Wednesday. Doth he feel it? No. Doth he hear it? No. 'Tis insensible, then? Yea, to the dead. But will it not live with the living? No. Why? Detraction will not suffer it. Therefore I'll none of it. Honour is a mere scutcheon – and so ends my catechism.

(V. 1. 131–40)

In *Henry IV, Part 2* Falstaff again epitomizes the 'wrong' choice for the Prince, while the Lord Chief Justice represents order and good government.

Many writers have pointed out that this structure goes back to the structure of the religious Morality plays. *Everyman*, in which good and evil qualities become characters in the drama and compete for the soul of man, is one of the most famous examples of this old dramatic genre. One critic has described the theme of *Henry IV* as 'the contention between vice and virtue for the soul of a prince'. Though it would be a mistake to see Falstaff simply as an embodiment of vice – he is so much more than that – it is true that he brags and clowns like the Vices in some of the old Morality plays did, and that some of the situations in the play also recall the Moralities. 'In *The Nature of the Four Elements* (1519) Sensual Appetyte under the guise of Friendship tempts Humanyte to the tavern, and in *Lusty Juventus* (*c.* 1540) the age-old Hypocrisy incites Juventus (Youth) to lechery and self-indulgence.' The idea of a morality-structure is helpful in any consideration of the shape of the *Henry IV* plays.

Shakespeare's sources

One of Shakespeare's sources for the play of *Henry IV* was the *Chronicles* by the historian Holinshed. Here is Holinshed's account of the interview between Prince Hal and his father which leads to Hal's reformation.

The prince kneeling downe before his father said: Most redoubted and souereigne lord and father, I am at this time come to your presence as your liege man, and as your naturall sonne, in all things to be at your commandement. And where I vnderstand you haue in suspicion my demeanour against your grace, you know verie well, that if I knew any man within this realme, of whome you should stand in feare, my duetie were to punish that person, thereby to remooue that greefe from your heart. Then how much more ought I to suffer death, to ease your grace of that greefe which you haue of me, being your naturall sonne and liege man: and to that end I haue this daie made my selfe readie by confession and receiuing of the sacrament. And therefore I beseech you most redoubted lord and deare father, for the honour of God, to ease your heart of all such suspicion as you haue of me, and to dispatch me heere before your knees, with this same dagger, [and withall he de-liuered vnto the king his dagger, in all humble reuerence; adding further, that his life was not so deare to him, that he wished to liue one daie with his displeasure] and therefore in thus ridding me out of life, and your selfe from all suspicion, here in presence of these lords, and before God at the date of the generall judgement, I faithfullie protest clearlie to forgiue you.

The king mooued herewith, cast from him the dagger, and imbracing the prince kissed him, and with shedding teares confessed, that in deed he had him partlie in suspicion, though now (as he perceiued) not with iust cause, and therefore from thencefoorth no misreport should cause him to haue him in mistrust, and this he promised of his honour. So by his great wisedome was the wrongfull suspicion which his father had conceiued against him remooued, and he restored to his fauour.

The legend of 'Madcap Hal'

When Shakespeare came to write about the youth of Henry V, he had a lot of popular stories to draw on. Many of the stories went back to the days of Henry V himself, and some were recorded in history books published later. Fabyan's *Chronicle*, published in 1516 described the Prince as full of 'all vice and insolence' and his companions as 'rioters and wild disposed persons', but told how, on coming to the throne, 'suddenly he became a new man' and banished his old friends from his presence. There were stories of the Prince actually striking the Lord Chief Justice of that time and being sent to prison, and accounts of him joining in highway robbery. A play called *The Famous Victories of Henry V*, which was probably written and performed two or three years before Shakespeare's *Henry IV*, contained all of these incidents. The disguised Prince and his gang robbed the king's taxmen, and Prince Henry was shown getting drunk at Eastcheap and throwing his tankard at a wall. Shakespeare's play uses a lot of the same traditional material, but never shows Hal as the drunken hooligan that some of the legends or the *Famous Victories* made him out to be. Shakespeare's picture of him is closer to that given by the historian Holinshed:

Indeed he was youthfullie giuen, growne to audacitie, and had chosen him companions agreeable to his age; with whome he spent the time in such recreations, exercises, and delights as he fansied. But yet (it should seeme by the report of some writers) that his behaviour was not offensiue or at least tending to the damage of anie bodie; sith he had a care to auoid dooing of wrong . . .

The comic plot

I cannot help thinking that there is more of contrivance and care in the execution of this play than in almost any he has written.
                                        (Elizabeth Montagu, 1769)

At first glance, *Henry IV, Part 1* seems to have two plots with very little to connect them. One is historic, public and serious, and concerns the rebellion of the Percy family and their alliance with the Welsh and Scottish rebels against the King. The other is comic, intimate and relaxed, and concerns Prince Hal, Falstaff, and the other regulars at the Boar's Head Tavern, Eastcheap, and their fooling. But the two plots have many links even though they exist independently, and it is impossible to imagine either of them unsupported by the other. The comic plot mirrors and mocks the historic plot continually, and really adds up to a sort of commentary on it.

'The Troublesome Reign of King Henry IV' is troublesome for the King on two levels. On the level of the historic plot, his reign is regularly punctuated by rebellions, and he has only to quell one for another to flare up in a different part of the kingdom. On the level of the comic plot, the King is troubled by the wild behaviour of the Prince of Wales, and by his apparent indifference to affairs of state and to his future position as King. Both of these troubles are stated clearly in the very first scene of the play. Both are (temporarily) settled by the battle of Shrewsbury, where the Percys' rebel forces are conquered and where Hal redeems his reputation on the battlefield.

The main theme of the historic plot is war and chivalry. Hotspur, the star of the historic plot, is held up as a rival to Hal, and it is his single-minded pursuit of military honour that makes him so admired. The comic plot continually questions and comments on the assumptions behind the heroic attitudes struck by the characters of the historic plot. Falstaff's speech on honour at Shrewsbury recalls Hotspur's earlier outburst on the same theme. On the road to Shrewsbury, Falstaff's speech revealing how he has managed to scrape together his tatty company of soldiers comes just after the scene where we have heard Vernon's ecstatic description of the Prince of Wales and his companions in their glittering armour.

The climax of the historic plot is the battle of Shrewsbury, where the characters put their courage to the test on the field of war. The climax of the comic plot is the Gad's Hill robbery, where courage and cowardice are also tested, but where the most important thing is to be able to outwit your companions and have a laugh at their expense.

The comic plot often parodies the historic plot. Just after the scene where Hotspur has taken his gruff leave of Lady Percy comes the tavern scene, where Hal makes fun of Hotspur and exactly mimics the tone of the scene we have just seen:

'O my sweet Harry,' says she, 'how many hast thou killed today?' 'Give my roan horse a drench,' says he, and answers, 'Some fourteen,' an hour after, 'a trifle, a trifle.'

(II. 4. 103–7)

The characters of the comic plot drop readily into play-acting to send up serious events. The most famous parody is the scene where Falstaff and the Prince take turns to play the King interviewing Hal about his bad habits and unsuitable companions. This is a parody that actually comes before the scene that it relates to in the historic plot.

Poised between the historic plot and the comic plot stands Prince Hal. In both plots he triumphs. He can fool as well as any man in Eastcheap and, in the Gad's Hill 'action' he thoroughly outwits Falstaff. In the battle of Shrewsbury he reveals himself as a shining example of chivalry, and wins all Hotspur's glories from him in their fight. His position as the main figure uniting the two plots confirms him as the central character of the play.

Falstaff

Falstaff is one of the richest characters that Shakespeare ever created. Here A. C. Bradley tries to analyse his charm:

The main reason why he makes us so happy and puts us so entirely at our ease is that he himself is happy and entirely at his ease. 'Happy' is too weak a word; he is in bliss, and we share his glory. Enjoyment – no fitful pleasure crossing a dull life, nor any vacant convulsive mirth – but a rich deep-toned chuckling enjoyment circulates continually through all his being. If you ask *what* he enjoys, no doubt the answer is, in the first place, eating and drinking, taking his ease at his inn, and the company of other merry souls. Compared with these things, what we count the graver interests of life are nothing to him. But then, while we are under his spell, it is impossible to consider these graver interests; gravity is to us, as to him, inferior to gravy; and what he does enjoy he enjoys with such a luscious and good-humoured zest that we sympathize and he makes us happy. And if any one objected, we should answer with Sir Toby Belch, 'Dost thou think, because thou art virtuous, there shall be no more cakes and ale?'

But this, again, is far from all. Falstaff's ease and enjoyment are not simply those of the happy man of appetite; they are those of the humorist, and the humorist of genius. Instead of being comic to you and serious to himself, he is more ludicrous to himself than to you; and he makes himself out more ludicrous than he is, in order that he and others may laugh. Prince Hal never made such sport of Falstaff's person as he himself did. It is *he* who says that his skin hangs about him like an old lady's loose gown, and that he walks before his page like a sow that hath o'erwhelmed all her litter but one. And he jests at himself when he is alone just as much as when others are by. It is the same with his appetites. The direct enjoyment they bring him is scarcely so great as the enjoyment of laughing at this enjoyment; and for all his addiction to sack you never see him for an instant with a brain dulled by it, or a temper turned solemn, silly, quarrelsome, or pious. The virtue it instils into him, of filling his brain with nimble, fiery, and delectable shapes – this, and his humorous attitude towards it, free him, in a manner, from slavery to it; and it is this freedom, and no secret longing for better things (those who attribute such a longing to him are far astray), that makes his enjoyment contagious and prevents our sympathy with it from being disturbed.

The bliss of freedom gained in humour is the essence of Falstaff. His humour is not directed only or chiefly against obvious absurdities; he is the enemy of everything that would interfere with his ease, and therefore of anything serious, and especially of everything respectable and moral. For these things impose limits and obligations, and make us the subjects of old father antic the law, and the categorical imperative, and our station and its duties, and conscience, and reputation, and other people's opinions, and all sorts of nuisances. I say he is therefore their enemy; but I do him wrong; to say that he is their enemy implies that he regards them as serious and recognizes their power, when in truth he refuses to recognize them at all. They are to him absurd; and to reduce a thing *ad absurdum* is to reduce it to nothing and to walk about free and rejoicing. This is what Falstaff does with all the would-be serious things of life, sometimes only by his words, sometimes by his actions too. He will make truth appear absurd by solemn statements, which he utters with perfect gravity and which he expects nobody to believe; and honour, by demonstrating that it cannot set a leg, and that neither the living nor the dead can possess it; and law, by evading all the attacks of its highest representative and almost forcing him to laugh at his own defeat; and patriotism, by filling his pockets with the bribes offered by competent soldiers who want to escape service, while he takes in their stead the halt and maimed and the gaol-birds; and duty, by showing how he labours in his vocation – of thieving; and courage, alike by mocking at his own capture of Colvile and gravely claiming to have killed Hotspur; and war, by offering the Prince his bottle of sack when he is asked for a sword; and religion, by amusing himself with remorse at odd times when he has nothing else to do; and the fear of death, by maintaining perfectly untouched, in the face of imminent peril and even while he *feels* the fear of death, the very same power of dissolving it in persiflage that he shows when he sits at ease in his inn. These are the wonderful achievements which he performs, not with the discontent of a cynic, but with the gaiety of a boy. And, therefore, we praise him, we laud him, for he offends none but the virtuous, and denies that life is real or life is earnest, and delivers us from the oppression of such nightmares, and lifts us into the atmosphere of perfect freedom.

(A. C. Bradley, 'The Rejection of Falstaff', from *Oxford Lectures on Poetry*, 1909)